PRAISE FOR *GROOMED*

"In *Groomed* Elizabeth shares a raw, heart-wrenching story, digging deeply to save others—a vital education, a sad tale, and a miracle of truth. Stopping sex trafficking and helping young women thrive is only possible through the education this book provides. And, ultimately, the sad realization that it could have been any of us!"

—DINA BAIR MAHER, WGN-TV, CHICAGO, ANCHOR/REPORTER

"Elizabeth Melendez Fisher Good shines a bright light on practical steps anyone can implement to dispel the darkness from which they have become enslaved. The first step, Good says, is to make a conscious decision to identify the grooming. She then leads the way to break free from the story that has been penned. Freedom is a journey, not an event, and it begins with selah."

—TAMELA J. YOUNG, MACM, ONE HEART ONE HOPE COACH; HEART2HEART SISTERHOOD FOUNDER/DIRECTOR

"In a world where women tend to define their worth by their appearance, often feel invisible, and frequently make decisions out of fear, the message of *Groomed* is desperately needed. Through her story, Elizabeth exposes the lies that groomed these destructive mind-sets in us and guides us to the truth of our true beauty, strength, and power. This book will change how you see yourself and other women, as Elizabeth shares solution-oriented insights with an authentic voice and great wisdom. She will inspire and equip you to live a life of purpose, satisfaction, and joy."

—KATHERINE LEE, PURE HOPE FOUNDATION FOUNDER AND AUTHOR, *INTERRUPTED*

"I'm incredibly moved by how God has used Elizabeth's story. The parts Satan meant to use to destroy her, God has used for good. Elizabeth is a warrior and champion giving a voice to the voiceless. *Groomed* is yet another way of helping those who can't or don't know how to help themselves. I am of the firm belief that everyone who reads this book will benefit in some way!"

—CINDY PENTECOST, IT WORKS! GLOBAL COFOUNDER AND AUTHOR, *I GET TO PREPARE MY HEART: A CHRISTMAS DEVOTIONAL*

"*Groomed* provides both women and men with insights and observations to help them increase their self-knowledge. With that knowledge their eyes can be opened to the influences that have shaped their lives for good and for ill. With that knowledge choices can be made to restore their lives and strengthen relationships as they were meant to be."

—QUIN FRAZER, DRINKER BIDDLE & REATH LLP PARTNER

"*Groomed* is an incredible, brave, and gorgeous book. It exposes, with loving wisdom, the spectrum of cruelties that do so much harm to so many while it also reveals the enduring capacity of love and truth, helping to lead people from victimization, through healing, and into a place where they can thrive. This book is not for the faint of heart but for anyone who wants to care more effectively for themselves or others; it has bountiful wisdom that will make the journey worth it."

—KAETHE MORRIS HOFFER, CHICAGO ALLIANCE AGAINST SEXUAL EXPLOITATION EXECUTIVE DIRECTOR

"This book is timely and speaks to all—male and female, young and old. Elizabeth's heart is poured into this book, not only to comfort the hurting but also to provide lifesaving help for those who have been hiding. Her personal story also offers guidance in recognizing those who need help. *Groomed* should be required reading for everyone in the counseling, teaching, health, and law enforcement fields."

—MARY LOU JOHNSON, LICENSED CLINICAL FAMILY THERAPIST AND AUTHOR/PHOTOGRAPHER, *THE LURE OF LONGBOAT KEY: SUNRISE TO SUNSET*

"Never are the marginalized more exploited than in times of prosperity. The bounty of some often comes through the trauma of others. In the modern Western world, we seek entertainment and distraction to patch the void left unfilled by the comforts of our times. *Groomed* reveals in heartbreaking anecdote after heartbreaking anecdote what it means to 'come to oneself,' to see the image of God within our fellow human beings. Elizabeth weaves a poetic narrative that exemplifies her belief that as we respect God's temple (the bodies of others), we give honor to our own temples, thus living in communion with God and with one another."

—STEVE BYNUM, WBEZ, CHICAGO

"*Groomed* is an amazingly bold and vulnerable look into the life of Elizabeth Melendez Fisher Good. In a powerful way Elizabeth allows us to enter her journey of pain with an incredible redemptive outcome. Lives will be changed as a result of her honesty. She has taken her tumultuous early years and turned them into a beautiful catalyst for good."

—ALAN SMYTH, SAVING INNOCENCE EXECUTIVE DIRECTOR

"*Groomed* is a captivating must-read for empowering women to take time to reflect on pervasive areas of our pasts and begin to step out and move beyond what we were groomed to be. As I read this book, I could feel the weight of my past lifting off. Elizabeth gives riveting, action-packed steps on how we can truly grasp a future full of freedom to be all we were created to be, walking stronger in the light of our new day."

—VALERIE ELLERY, INTERNATIONAL INSPIRATIONAL AUTHOR, SPEAKER, AND HUMAN TRAFFICKING EDUCATION SPECIALIST

"Elizabeth Melendez Fisher Good allows us to witness a life full of secrets, survival, and resilience. *Groomed* is full of important information for those of us who want to enjoy the companionship of our best selves and those we serve in the world of social services."

—DR. STEPHANIE POWELL, JOURNEY OUT EXECUTIVE DIRECTOR; RETIRED, LOS ANGELES POLICE DEPARTMENT

GROOMED

GROOMED

*Escaping the Messages of Your Past
and Taking Charge of Your Future*

ELIZABETH MELENDEZ FISHER GOOD

with Beth Jusino

W PUBLISHING GROUP

AN IMPRINT OF THOMAS NELSON

Published in Nashville, Tennessee, by W Publishing Group, an imprint of Thomas Nelson.

The author is represented by MacGregor Literary, Inc.

Thomas Nelson titles may be purchased in bulk for educational, business, fund-raising, or sales promotional use. For information, please email SpecialMarkets@ThomasNelson.com.

Scripture quotations are taken from the ESV® Bible (The Holy Bible, English Standard Version®). © 2001 by Crossway, a publishing ministry of Good News Publishers. Used by permission. All rights reserved.

The names and identifying characteristics of certain individuals have been changed to protect their privacy.

Any Internet addresses, phone numbers, or company or product information printed in this book is offered as a resource and is not intended in any way to be or to imply an endorsement by Thomas Nelson, nor does Thomas Nelson vouch for the existence, content, or services of these sites, phone numbers, companies, or products beyond the life of this book.

ISBN 978-0-7852-2970-4 (eBook)

Library of Congress Control Number: 2019032798

ISBN 978-0-7852-2966-7 (TP)

Printed in the United States of America

20 21 22 23 24   LSC   10 9 8 7 6 5 4 3 2 1

*To my three beautiful children—Sammi, Max, and Leo—
with my deepest love and gratitude. I am in awe of who you
each are, groomed for authenticity. Always speak the truth!*

And to my precious husband, Mr. Good. My heart overflows.

CONTENTS

CONTENTS

INTRODUCTION

How Did I End Up Here?

It started with a secret.

Something happened when she was a child, right under the watchful eye of her mother. Something that she couldn't tell anyone about.

Someone she trusted did something to her body that she couldn't forget. It changed the way she forever saw herself.

That secret festered and stuck with her, and soon she'd collected more. If she told the truth to anyone now, she thought, she would be dismissed, judged—or worse. So she stayed quiet. She gave up her voice because there was too much she couldn't say. A shell of protectiveness covered her once-bright personality.

Then another person came into her life and said the words she longed to hear.

I love you.

I'll take care of you.

I see you.

That person led her into places she never thought she'd go. Convinced her to do things she never thought she'd do. Told her to sell herself because that's all she was good for. Until, finally, she started to believe . . .

She was worthless.

She didn't deserve to live a full life.

What had happened would define her forever.

So she stayed in the places that risked her body and tore at her soul.

The story above could describe any of the eighteen hundred young women a year who come through the doors of Selah Freedom, the organization I cofounded almost ten years ago. They are the survivors of sex trafficking, the heartbreaking $150 billion per year industry that takes children—in America, usually runaways—and coerces them into business transactions where they're forced to have sex as often as forty times a day.

But rather than describing their lives, which are unimaginable to most of us, I've shared a piece of *my* story.

That might surprise you if you saw me in the grocery store or school carpool line. I probably look a lot like you. I'm a mom with a master's degree, three teenagers, and no police record. I never walked the streets or took money for sex. Yet I've had my share of secrets, abuse, and even groomers.

No, I'm not talking about the stereotypical pimps you see

on TV—the ones who wear feathered purple hats and fur coats, lingering on street corners and luring vulnerable girls into back seats and hotel rooms. My groomers were subtler, but they still manipulated my young, impressionable soul, filling my head with lies they claimed were "for my own good." They taught me to do things to benefit themselves, not unlike the ways in which the stereotypical pimps we encounter at Selah Freedom groom girls (and sometimes boys) to send out to the street.

I let my groomers' messages define me and my actions for decades. I let them lead me into compromises because I thought I didn't deserve anything more. I settled for less. I lost my voice and my sense of self.

I let myself be controlled by the secrets and lies, and they did a number on me. It's taken more than forty years to unravel my thoughts and actions, and still today, even in the process of writing this book, I'm uncovering new things.

And you know what else? I'm not alone. The more I talk to women across the country—from every kind of background you can imagine—the more I realize we've all been groomed for some kind of future. Far too often it's a future we never would have chosen for ourselves.

But no more. For years adults in power have taken advantage of young, vulnerable women, and the world is waking up to just how much we have endured. Headlines and hashtags blast the stories of other bold women tired of hiding in the shadows. From the entertainment industry to the workplace and even the church, painful scandals have rocked the status quo.

It's time to bring light into darkness.

This move toward honesty is not a fad, and it's not going away. Many of you know firsthand what those women on the news are talking about. Research shows one out of three women in America was sexually abused during childhood.[1] No matter how many years it's been, if that's your story, those scars are probably still with you. Women who experienced sexual abuse or assault, especially those who never told anyone, are more likely to struggle with depression, eating disorders, anxiety, and shame. They're also more likely to enter abusive adult relationships.[2] The voices of those early groomers are always with us.

But even if that's not part of your story, this book is for you. Women today have been groomed for a lot more than just sex.

Have you ever wondered, *How did I end up here?* Do past hurts pop up regularly to squelch your happiness and limit your opportunities? Do you feel stuck in a life that looks good on the surface but leaves you unfulfilled? Or are you struggling under the weight of relationships and expectations that don't seem to fit your deepest heart longings?

No one wants to believe they have been controlled or sold out by someone they trusted. But chances are, you were groomed to live for something other than your true self, and the more years you spend in that false place, the more uncomfortable and smothering it feels.

I'm writing this book to help you move past the place where you're currently stuck. No one has to be defined by their past. No one has to live for their groomers. But to get there, we need to take a giant, scary step back and look at where we came from and why we believe certain things about ourselves. We need to identify the ways we have been groomed.

It won't be easy. I'm going to ask you to uncover some of your deepest secrets, look at them honestly in the light of day, and ask questions about the motives of the people closest to you.

You may shed a lot of tears as you read, and you'll probably have some hard conversations. But in the end, if you stick with me, you'll discover a new way of living—one that brings light into the dark corners of your life and allows you to discover a way forward in fullness and freedom.

Are you ready?

Part 1

↵

WE'VE ALL BEEN GROOMED

Chapter 1

THE SECRETS WE KEEP

One summer evening when I was six years old, my sister, Diana, tucked me in and kissed me good night, just like she always did. Diana was nine years older than me, and she was my nurturer—the one who cuddled me, dressed me for Halloween, and played games with me. She was my hero.

Our seventeen-year-old brother was down the hall in his room, putting away his hunting rifle. Our mom grew up in a rural area where hunting was a normal part of life, and her kids all learned how to handle weapons safely, so the accident that followed should never have happened. But it did.

As Diana passed the open doorway to my brother's room, the gun misfired. The bullet struck her temple and killed her instantly.

I slept through the chaos that happened next—the sirens, the paramedics, the pools of blood, the cries of my family members. Looking back, it's clear that my ability to black out during traumatic situations started early.

I went to sleep with a beloved sister. When I woke up, she had disappeared. But the real tragedy for me was that no one in my house ever talked about Diana again—at least not to me. In grief, everyone went dark.

My parents sheltered me from the aftermath of the accident. I stayed with relatives for two weeks while the house was scrubbed and my sister was buried. I wasn't allowed to go to the funeral. I know that it was all done to protect me, but the result was that I never had the chance to say goodbye.

Years later a family friend told me about Diana's funeral. Close to a thousand people filled the church until it was standing room only. I think about that day often and wish I could have seen such an outpouring. It would have matched what I was feeling. Instead, I was alone. Nothing in my external world acknowledged the level of my internal grief, and I was left with so many questions. I sometimes felt as if I had imagined having a sister. As if she had been a dream.

A few weeks after Diana's death, I went with my family to a cousin's wedding. There was an empty space in the line of bridesmaids where Diana was supposed to stand, but still no one mentioned her.

After the ceremony a family member found me crying in a corner. "What's wrong?" she asked.

"I miss Diana," I whimpered. My stiff, ruffled dress crumpled around me. My loss in that moment was achingly physical. I longed for my sister. I wanted to talk about her, to cry to someone, to grieve.

Instead of opening her arms to me, my relative said, "You're not even old enough to remember her." Then she walked away.

The message was clear: My grief was not welcome in my family. I would have to hold this deep ache inside.

It was my first secret.

❧

What was your first secret? You know, that thing in your past, probably in your childhood, that forever altered the way you understood everything?

Before your first secret, you thought the world was safe and your place in it was assured. But secrets shift that perception. They make things seem out of balance. When people you thought you could trust reveal themselves as flawed, your future becomes a little less hopeful.

The memory of your first secret probably still stings, even after all these years. It's not pleasant to talk about. Perhaps someone warned you never to talk about it. Yet it's never far away. It reaches into your life even now. It comes to your mind when you're alone, without distractions.

More than forty years after Diana died, I still think about my sister every day.

Who do you think about?

Our painful secrets are as diverse as we are, and so are the results. They emerge from moments of trauma, whether those come from accidents, negligence, or the intentional actions of others. For me, grief was my first secret. For others, it was a feeling of being unloved or unwanted. I know women who hold secrets about the first time they lied to cover for a loved one's issues or the first time someone shamed them for being different from everyone else.

For the survivors who come to Selah Freedom, their secrets were almost always what drove them from their homes. Running away was preferable to being crushed by the weight of their unspoken burdens.

I've never met a person—man or woman, wealthy or scraping by, married or single, in a faith community or not—who hasn't covered over some kind of wound.

And yet we all assume that since everyone around us seems fine, we're alone in our pain.

I'm here to say that, no, we're not alone.

Things went downhill fast for my family after Diana died. My brother enlisted in the military and left home as soon as he turned eighteen. I understand now why he did it, but at the time it seemed like he, too, disappeared from my young life. Then my father's job transferred him from Chicago to California, and my parents explained that he would move alone at first "to settle in." I was too young to understand what the trauma of losing a child had done to their already rocky marriage. Within a few months my noisy, active household of five shrunk to just my mom and me, living alone with our secrets.

My mother has always been stoic, quiet, and task oriented; I take after my father's emotional, confrontational, relational nature. I remember those years with her as being very quiet, my mother and I each going about our own lives. I longed for the chaos and action that had once filled my home. I ached for Diana and her emotional covering and caretaking.

It's no surprise, then, that my favorite childhood memories

happened in the summers, when we would visit my mother's family in Arkansas. My aunts and uncles lived on farms in the country, in places so rural that some didn't even have running water. It was a paradise for a city kid like me. I had lots of cousins to play with and could ride horses and name baby animals.

The summer I turned twelve, though, another dark cloud entered my life—and it happened in the one place where I still felt like a safe, protected child.

Everyone was getting ready for church on a Sunday morning, and I was fixing my hair in the bathroom. One of the adults who was often around—not an immediate family member, but a family friend—came into the room and stood behind me, staring at me in the mirror.

"You've really grown up this year," he told me. "You're so pretty now." Then he reached around me and put his hands on my breasts.

I froze. I couldn't speak. I couldn't move. My only thought was, *This can't be happening.*

And then he was gone, walking out of the bathroom as casually as he'd walked in.

The moment felt unreal. This was someone I'd known my entire life, someone I trusted. He wouldn't do something like that! I finished getting ready and tried to push away the memory, ignoring the new sensations of shame I felt in my body.

When the family split up into different cars to head to church, the man arranged for me to ride with him. I didn't argue; who would believe me if I revealed what he'd done? I watched with detached terror as he slid his hand under my long, conservative skirt. I can still see the look he gave me, not one of lust but of pure power.

When we got to church, that same man pulled out a guitar and headed inside to the front, a smile on his face. He was on the worship team.

While my molester sang about Jesus, I went to the bathroom and cried. All I felt was confusion. What had happened seemed like something from a soap opera, not my normal Christian family life. It was too big, too damaging for me to take in.

By the time I went back to the service, I knew that I could never tell anyone what had happened. Another secret.

When the music ended and we all sat down in the pews, one of my uncles put his arm around me, probably sensing that I was uneasy. My family was always physically affectionate, and the day before, I would have leaned into him and accepted his comfort. But that morning I pulled away as if he'd shocked me. From that moment forward, for years, I could never relax or find physical comfort in a man's touch.

I was on guard the rest of that summer. When my mom and I finally left for Chicago, I told her I didn't ever want to come back. She never questioned why.

Far too often a person's early secrets include sexual abuse at the hands of a relative or trusted person—the ultimate betrayal against someone too innocent and vulnerable to respond.

Perhaps it happened once. Perhaps it happened over and over. Maybe a family member came into a child's bedroom late at night. Maybe a coach asked a player to stay after practice. Maybe it was a babysitter. Maybe it was a family friend. The perpetrators are all different, but their message is almost always the same: "Don't tell anyone. No one will believe you."

So the crime becomes another secret that festers. Research from the American Counseling Association shows that once a girl has been violated, her sense of worth plummets, and her sense of her own body changes.[1] In the years I've worked with victims of sex trafficking, I haven't met a single girl who entered "the life" who wasn't first abused sexually.

But even those who escape this outcome of sexual exploitation are often not truly free of their pasts. I've met hundreds of abused women who went on to become mothers, wives, and professionals. They are running the world and raising the next generation—all while burdened by memories of unacknowledged sexual abuse.

That changes a person over time. Carrying secrets hurts us mentally, emotionally, and even physically. Unaddressed trauma stays in the body and builds. In fact, one well-publicized study from 2012 shows that living with secrets makes us feel physically heavier.[2] In turn, tackling the stresses and challenges of normal life becomes harder. And secrets don't only affect the person holding them. They radiate out and, if left unaddressed, almost always are passed down. Sexual abuse, especially, is generational, and the courage to speak about it to our kids carries great power to end it.

I have had mothers ask me to meet with their daughters. Their stories are often similar. The girls' behaviors have changed. They've become promiscuous and are left in risky situations. In most cases when I talk with these girls, I discover they have been raped in a social situation and have internalized it. They feel it was their fault; they could have tried harder to stop it.

When they have let others know what happened, nothing is done. The guy is too popular, or she must have led him on. Why was she out that late, in that situation?

The girls are ashamed and devastated. They believe their reputations are ruined. So the next time boys at a party pushed them for more, they reasoned, why not? *I've already been used, so what does it matter?*

After these conversations, I speak with the mothers, many of whom I know have been abused. I always ask if they have shared their secret with their children. Again and again the answer is no; they carried too much shame, were afraid what their children would think of them. When not shared openly, these secrets become the same burden the next generation carries. That which is kept in the dark grows and infects the family line. But that which is brought into the light is dispelled.

Even though I never saw that man from Arkansas again, what he did to me affected my ability to trust others for decades. Not only did I treat men differently, but the way I felt about church and safe communities changed too. It also started me on a journey that eventually led to where I am today. Now, when survivors of sex trafficking talk to me about their lives, I understand. When they act tough, with a shell that's a mile thick and an it's-no-big-deal attitude, I get it. And when I open myself and show them where I've been, the walls of their secrets start to come down.

When I was in graduate school, one of my psychology professors explained that when a person's worldview shatters, it rarely happens with a single lightning bolt. Instead, the things we believe break down a little bit at a time, as one disappointment after another leaves us cracked and changed.

About a year after that last summer in Arkansas, my mother told me she and my father were divorcing. Because my mom was hurt, she shared far more than she should have about the reasons for the breakup. No middle school girl needs to know the details of her parents' marriage.

My whole world felt like it was rocking on its axis, and as soon as that school year ended, I retreated for a long, healing visit with other extended family members. My aunt and uncle lived in central Illinois with my cousin, who was close to my age. Unlike most of my father's social, expressive, and exuberant family, this aunt and uncle were quiet, intentional, and newly sober. Their house was a respite; whenever I visited, I knew they would sit and really listen to me. I felt safe when I was with them.

But that refuge, too, would crumble.

One night my cousin and I went to a teen dance club not far from the local university. This was what kids in the '80s did, and it was usually innocent and fun. But that night one of the bouncers at the club noticed us and asked if we wanted to go to his college frat party instead.

Who would say no to that? Not two young girls who loved to dance.

The bouncer told us to go home and put on "something to look older" before we came over. In our naïveté we decided that meant we should raid my aunt and uncle's closet. I still remember how I styled my uncle's peach-and-blue-checked shirt—tied at my waist, blue beads wrapped around my neck. I was nervous, but my cousin seemed so cool and confident that I believed nothing could go wrong.

Looking back, I wonder if she was scared, too, and counting on me to know how to handle the situation. We both were way out of our league.

As soon as we got to the party, a frat guy swooped in on us. While I can still picture his white muscle shirt and black parachute pants, his name didn't stick—perhaps because right away he offered us drinks from his red Igloo cooler full of Jack and Coke.

I took one and then another. I'd grown up around alcohol at family parties and get-togethers but personally had never had more than a stolen sip or two. It didn't take long for me to get blackout drunk.

The next thing I remember is my cousin dragging me out of a bedroom that had no door while I tried clumsily to pull my clothes back on. There was blood on the sheets.

I was fourteen, a churchgoing girl who my friends all joked would be the last person in our group to have sex. I would be on the pill and use a condom on my wedding night, they said. But here I was, barely in high school and no longer a virgin. That faceless, nameless frat guy had finished what the Arkansas worship leader started the year before.

Another huge part of me died when I was raped.

Back at the party, I could tell that my cousin was disgusted with the guy and with me. Through the haze of alcohol, I felt the beginnings of shame but pushed it away. I knew that if I let myself feel the depth of this secret, it would eat me alive.

"What's the big deal?" I asked. "It's nothing." Then I invited my rapist to come hang out with us for the rest of the night.

It took me years of hearing similar stories from other women to realize my reaction that night—pretending everything was normal—is common after a rape, especially one that happens in a social setting. Far too many of us believe that the secret to healing is to bury our secrets.

⤺

Can you share your secret?

Maybe not yet. But I bet that if you and I sat down for a cup of coffee, face-to-face, and you let me talk for a while, eventually a secret would come out. I have that effect on people. I can't tell you how many times I've heard someone say, "I've never told anyone this before, but . . ."

At first I thought it was weird. *Why was everyone telling me all this?* But I've come to realize that their openness is a reflection of my own. I don't have secrets anymore. I've spent the last couple of decades doing a lot of soul searching and getting whole and healed. At some point I realized I had to stop holding back the truth about the things that hurt me. Today my life is on the table for anyone to see. I've told my stories to my kids. I've told them to my parents. I've shared them on national media outlets and with young women rebuilding their lives after surviving sex trafficking. I've told random strangers at cocktail parties.

My brutal, total transparency about everything encourages others to share their own stories. I am always amazed at the secrets still tucked deeply away.

I've sat with a seventy-year-old woman, an elder in her church, who tearfully told me about the seven abortions she had when she was young, and the sexual abuse that happened before that. She carried the secret with her for more than fifty years, not even telling her husband. I've wept with the wife of a high-profile CEO as she described the bruises her husband was careful to leave only behind her hairline, where they wouldn't show when she accompanied him to expensive fund-raisers.

No one's life, it turns out, is as perfect as what we imagine for them. We all have something in our pasts that we try to push into a corner, dark things we try not to mention.

But if I've learned anything from my experiences as a woman, a daughter, a mother, a counselor, and a thought leader, it's that we all need to talk more about our secrets. We need to throw open the doors and let light shine in. Sharing the uncomfortable and even the ugly parts of our stories is the most beautiful and powerful gift we can offer one another because when one person speaks truth, it frees others to follow.

Yes, that kind of transparency is scary, especially if your secret is tied to a memory or feeling you've been holding on to for a long time. It may feel like offering your secret gives others the power to hurt you. But the opposite is true.

When we bury our secrets and refuse to acknowledge the painful pieces of our past because of fear or shame, they hold power over us and weigh us down.

When we sacrifice the right to speak our own truth, we're left vulnerable to the power and perceived opinions of others.

And as we allow others' opinions to fill us with even more doubts and questions about our true worth, things can quickly go from bad to worse.

Chapter 2

THE MESSAGES WE HEAR

Within forty-eight hours of leaving home, 80 percent of runaways are approached by a predator.[1]

He doesn't tell her he's a predator, of course. He says he's a friend—often her only friend, her rescuer. He offers her food. He lets her share what's on her mind. He compliments her.

He does whatever he has to do to gain her trust. It doesn't usually take much, after everything the girl has already experienced. Long before she met the man who will become her pimp, someone else left her convinced that she doesn't deserve intimacy or self-respect. By adding to that message and encouraging her dependence, this new guy can easily break down the last walls standing between her and the camera or the tricks on the street.

Before long the girl finds herself in situations that she never wanted to be in, but by then she thinks it's too late to turn back. She's groomed to believe he is the only person who will ever care about her, and she covers her inner turmoil because she believes she has no other options. No one else will ever love her like he does, if she can just gain his favor.

She takes on a new persona, an emotional shell to keep her safe. She's received the message loud and clear: abuse is all she deserves.

The summer I was fourteen, before I went to Illinois and met the boy in parachute pants who would change my life, I had a boyfriend. Let's call him Josh. He looked like a Greek god, tanned from spending his summer at the pool and muscled from wrestling team practices at our rival high school.

I spent as much time with Josh as possible, but since I was a "good Christian girl," I never let him go too far physically. He called me a prude, but he didn't break up with me.

Then I went to that frat party and came home a different person. I didn't tell my friends or family what had happened, but it would have been obvious to anyone paying attention that I was in some kind of crisis. The problem was, no one was paying attention.

Josh was out of town the weekend I went to my first high school party. There were some older boys there, seniors from Josh's school. The party scene made me nervous, and I got blackout drunk again. I don't remember anything that happened, but the next day, the story spread that I'd had sex with one of the varsity members of Josh's wrestling team. I probably did. Or rather, he had sex with me.

Josh, of course, was hurt and furious. He broke up with me. I begged him not to, but he wouldn't even speak to me.

To say I was heartbroken would be an understatement. I was a mess. I cried for four months. I think it was the first time I was allowed to grieve something, and so I grieved everything. I cried for Josh, for Diana, for the morning I was molested and the night I was raped.

By Christmas, when I was still crying every day, I told my mom I needed to see a psychiatrist. I'd continued going to parties even though every time I ended up so drunk I passed out. Thank God this was in the days before iPhone videos and social media, but someone from the party always called me the next day to tell me what had transpired. In a few months, I'd gone from "church girl" to "slut."

Today I'm well known for saying that there's no such thing as a seventh-grade slut; there's only a little girl who's been abused and lost her ability to say no. Once you believe that you've lost your worth, there's no point in trying to stand up for yourself anymore. But that kind of adult wisdom doesn't change the minds of the mean girls at school. My former friends almost all turned against me.

My mom, who had watched me fall apart with increasing but silent concern, set up an appointment with a counselor right away.

After a couple of conversations, my counselor grabbed a bottle of Coke and shook it up. "Right now," he said, "you're like this bottle. There's so much pressure inside you that if we try to unscrew the lid too fast, you'll burst all over the place. We're going to have to go slow and unscrew a tiny bit at a time so you can release what's inside little by little."

17

We all received messages that built up inside us when we were young. They came from our parents, our siblings, our friends, our teachers, and our enemies. Some of them were life-giving. *You are safe here. You are loved. I will help you. I respect you. You belong.*

Other messages, though, left lasting damage.

You're not pretty enough.

You're not smart enough.

You're not good enough.

You're broken.

You don't matter.

It's your fault.

That last one gets a lot of women I know, even the ones who look like rock stars from the outside. Despite being at the top of the business world or worthy of a mother-of-the-year award, they spend their lives moving in shame, always secretly believing that if anything goes wrong, it will be their fault because they're just not *enough*.

Where do those messages come from? And why are they so pervasive?

When we're young, our minds don't have the critical-thinking skills to process messages skeptically. Study after study shows that children intuitively believe what adults tell them, even if those messages contradict what they can see right in front of them.[2] Not only that, but children internalize those messages and carry them into adulthood. When boys are routinely complimented as smart and girls are told they're pretty, it affects what they seek in the future.

As a child, I believed that grief wasn't something to share and that I couldn't talk about what I'd lost. I believed that even though a year after Diana's death, when a cousin died in another tragic accident, I saw a totally different response. My aunt refused to let her son's name disappear. She celebrated my cousin every day and talked about him every chance she got.

"Would you like me to make you Danny's favorite breakfast?" she asked one morning when I was visiting. "I never get to make it anymore." I was stunned. My aunt showed me a powerful message of honor and love, but I still was stuck in what I thought I knew about silence and rejection.

How were you groomed? What message did your parents give you? For one of my friends, the message she most remembers is her mother's sharp and repeated criticism of her weight. She learned not only that her appearance mattered more than her inner self, but also that her appearance was disappointing. Another woman remembers the day a teacher in her preschool told her "girls don't do that" when she said she wanted to be a race car driver. Her dreams, she learned, were wrong. The way she saw herself was bad.

Plenty of messages come to us without words. When we're ignored, dismissed, rebuked, or treated differently than everyone else, the messages build, and our futures start to bend toward something that was never meant for us.

That psychiatrist with the Coke bottle was good for me, and I always wonder what would have happened if I'd stuck with our sessions. Would I have learned how to redirect my life? I'll never know because before we could unscrew the bottle cap very far, my path diverted.

My parents were divorced by then, and money was tight. When it was clear that we could no longer afford to live in our Chicago house, my mom decided we should move to Florida to be near my dad.

I didn't fight the move. I'd burned so many bridges and hurt my reputation so badly at my Chicago high school that it was a relief to think about starting over. Maybe in Florida I could become the church girl again.

But as the saying goes, *Wherever you go, there you are.*

The first weekend after we moved to our new home in Fort Lauderdale, some girls invited me to a party. I went, and, not surprisingly, I got drunk, blacked out, and the boyfriend of the most popular girl at my new high school had sex with me. My reputation was trashed before I even walked through the school doors.

I decided that if I couldn't be the church girl, I would be what everyone thought I was. For the rest of high school, I was the party girl, and I made it a game to hurt boys before they could hurt me. I would set my sights on someone and lure him in, get him to fall for me, and then cheat on him and break his heart. Looking back, there was not one person, male or female, who I cared about back then. How could I love others when I didn't love myself?

The rest of my life was a mess too. I went from being an honor student to barely passing my classes, and I got kicked off one sports team after another. Some of the football players I hung out with got involved with a Miami gang, and they started dealing drugs. Our lives were right out of a bad TV drama, with girls in bikinis passing off packets of cocaine on the beach for their boyfriends and people getting into fights on street corners.

My family worried about me, and a few tried to intervene. But I don't think it would have made a difference. I was drunk every chance I got, trying hard to be numb all the time. The result, unfortunately, was only more shame.

In my senior year of high school, I got pregnant. I didn't tell anyone except the father, who was officially my boyfriend, though we constantly cheated on each other. I never considered having the baby, even though I'd grown up in churches with strong pro-life messages. I had big plans for my life, and a baby didn't fit them. My boyfriend's uncle sent money from New Jersey, and I had an abortion. I didn't tell anyone about it for years.

Those early messages about the need to stay silent had burned deep into my brain and groomed me for secrets.

↞

What do you think about when you hear the word *groomed*?

Once upon a time being groomed wasn't a negative thing, and even today parents groom their children for the bright futures they want them to have. Wealthy families groom their sons and daughters for success by sending them to elite prep schools and Ivy League colleges and introducing them to the "right" people. Christian parents groom their children to believe in Jesus and serve the church. Mentors groom young adults to succeed in their careers. The children of farmers are groomed to one day take over the family business.

Today, though, the word has taken on darker meanings. We see *grooming* used mostly in headlines that refer to the intentional, methodical way that sexual predators and sociopaths manipulate others to take advantage of them.

These coercive behaviors are real, and they happen more often than most of us think, but they don't change the truth that everyone was groomed for something, and it all started with the messages we learned from the people we trusted.

The more time I spend working with survivors and hearing their stories, while also talking to friends, volunteers, donors, and women who have never been touched by sex trafficking or sexual abuse, the more I find common threads among us, and the more I understand how important it is not to let go of that original way we looked at grooming. There's a lot more to it than the stereotypical pimps, pornographers, and pedophiles.

The strongest influencers in your young life became your groomers. Sometimes intentionally, but often not, they changed the way you view yourself and your world, how you present yourself, where you feel secure and insecure, and even the choices you make years later as an adult.

I want to say this again: not all grooming is negative. Everything in our lives prepares us for something. If your parents valued travel and adventure, for example, and took you on exotic camping trips to South America and train rides across Europe, then you were likely groomed to have an openness to the world and a willingness to explore different cultures. If your parents preferred to stay close to home, spending vacations in familiar places within easy driving distance or not taking vacations at all, then you were probably groomed to have a sense of rootedness, commitment, and connection to a community.

In grad school I learned about the biopsychosocial model, which basically means that a person's mind, body, and culture are interconnected, and all three things influence our experiences. Human beings are complex creations, and what manifests as a physical problem often has social or psychological aspects, like a headache that's related to stress over a family conflict or an emotional outburst that's tied, in part, to an imbalance of hormones.

Our insides and outsides are connected, and our perspectives are influenced heavily by the society around us. That means that your parents, siblings, teachers, coaches, spiritual leaders, and others affect who you're attracted to, who you marry, your career choice, your parenting style, and, most of all, how you see yourself.

Am I saying that everything about who you are as an adult can be tied back to how you were raised? Of course not. The personality traits you were born with are the core of your being, and those are what define how you respond to your grooming. If you've raised more than one child, you know what I'm talking about. Our kids are born with personalities already intact, and by the time they're a few months old, you can start to see what those are. Of my own three kids, only my middle son was born with my natural ability or desire to spar. He'll argue with me all day long for no reason. His two siblings are nothing like that, even though they were all born within five years of each other and grew up in the same house, the same environment, with the same parents.

My brother and I were raised by the same parents who groomed us with the same mix of messages and emotions. Our core personalities responded in opposite ways. I'm an extrovert. I love big cities and activity and live a very social life. He, on the other hand, despises going downtown, preferring to stay close to home with a small circle of friends.

Who you really are, at your core, is entirely yours. But until you learn to look critically at how social messages have affected you and begin to challenge the ones that don't enhance your life, they'll keep leading you down the same disappointing, dark paths.

After the abortion, I wanted to get my life back together. I graduated high school, found a small Christian college far from all my bad influences, and told my mom that this was where I wanted to go. She loved the idea.

For the first six months of my freshman year, I kept myself together. I played volleyball and got good grades. I thought I was on track, but those messages from my past were still there. No matter how good I acted, I believed in my heart that I was broken.

Eventually the party crowd found me, and I couldn't say no. I got in trouble for dancing, which was against the rules at that school, and things went downhill. I started sneaking out and getting drunk. By the spring I was coaching the dean's daughter on how to lose her virginity. That, not surprisingly, was the end of my Christian college experience.

I wasn't giving up on my plans for a bigger life though. I'd set my sights on a career in broadcast journalism. After a brief stint at community college to get my grades together, I transferred to Purdue University in Indiana. I spent just one semester there before I found my way to Southern Illinois University, which had the best broadcast journalism program in the state.

By that point the partying life had gotten old. I was still drinking but not nearly as much or as often. I'd learned to control my blackouts, which also limited my random sexual encounters. By my senior year of college, my friends all called me Mom because I seemed so much older and more experienced than them. I'd lived hard and fast, and it was time to get serious about life.

In my senior year I received a competitive internship at a major TV network in Chicago, which turned into a job after graduation. I was making great money, living in the heart of the city, and going to church with my aunts and cousins every Sunday. My life looked great on the outside, but on the inside things were still a mess. As the pressure at work mounted, I added binge eating and compulsive shopping to the list of ways I numbed and covered my pain.

Mine was an exhausting double life, and on the surface I finally had all the things my parents wanted for me.

Then when I was twenty-six, I met the man who would become my husband. He was eleven years older than me, financially well-off, and groomed in all the ways that impressed me. Still, I played it cool. "Oh, you want to take me to a Bulls game? That's okay, I have season tickets of my own through work." "No thanks, I've been to that fancy restaurant already."

Looking back, I understand that my attitude, treating our relationship like a competition to win, should have been the first warning sign, but all I saw at the time was how much I had in common with this guy. Even the strip clubs.

Porn had been part of my life ever since I was six years old. Growing up, every house I visited seemed to have a *Playboy* magazine or two lying around. I had always been surrounded by short shorts, high heels, and plenty of cleavage because that's what the women in my extended family were told men wanted.

Not surprisingly, when my pain and confusion mixed with an environment like that, porn became another secret coping mechanism. It taught me to see sex as a power game, and I brought that to this new relationship.

Though it was our soul wounds, still open and bleeding, that fit each other, at the time it felt like completion—a very strong draw.

My husband proposed six weeks after we met, and we married nine months later. Over the next three years I quit my job and gave birth to our first child, and we moved from the city to Chicago's North Shore, one of the most affluent, exclusive neighborhoods in the entire country.

Porn and soul wounds remained a hidden yet consistent thread in my life, but for all outward appearances, this girl from a broken home had come a long way.

Have you ever heard the term *soul wounds*? It describes the deepest parts of a person's past that are still causing damage in the present. As long as a wound remains open and festering, it's going to attract the attention of others—those who have that same wound or those who want to take advantage of it. Until we heal our soul wounds, we become victims of them.

One of the most important messages we share with the girls who come through Selah Freedom is the need to challenge and shed their pasts. Until they do, they carry a vulnerability that makes them susceptible to those who may take advantage of them in the future. Until they can see themselves from their grooming, it's as if they're wearing bumper stickers on their foreheads that say "I am a victim. Use me. Take advantage of me."

For many of us it takes an outside voice to draw our attention to what we've been living with for far too long. At different times in my life when I've talked to friends about what was happening, someone has tilted her head at just the right angle and asked, "And are you okay with that?"

That's a powerful question, and it's often a hard one to answer. Because, sure, for a long time we've learned to be okay with whatever it is. The neglect. The abuse. The resentment. The unforgiveness. We've made so many excuses and learned to live with so much less that it feels normal. Until someone comes along with a fresh perspective. Someone who can see how much we're missing. Someone brave enough to ask.

Are you okay with that?

Chapter 3

THE STORIES WE TELL

When I travel the country to speak about Selah Freedom, the people I talk to have a variety of reactions. Some get angry on behalf of our girls and envision taking on the traffickers. They speak up and demand justice for the unimaginable.

In every crowd, though, plenty of other people get very quiet. They close their eyes to hide the tears that well up. Those tender souls, I've learned, are not shocked by the difficult lives of girls trapped in sex trafficking. They're all too aware of how a girl could feel desperate to the point of believing she deserves the terrible things that happen to her. They are reliving their own, sometimes deeply hidden, pasts.

There's a good chance that you, as you're reading this, also find yourself with one of two reactions. Some of you have already seen yourself in my story. These chapters have made you think about your own abuse, grief, or difficult relationships. You're deeply, painfully aware of the messages you carried into adulthood because they still echo in your head every day. If so, keep reading. My deepest desire is that this book helps you find healing.

But if you're not sure about this idea of grooming yet, stick with me. If you suspect that this book is about *them* but not *you*, keep reading. Because even if there's not a secret living on the surface that you think about every day, I guarantee there's a part of you that's been groomed, and understanding what that is will unleash you into a life that may surpass your wildest dreams.

The memories and messages of our pasts affect us, creeping up slowly and building into years of compromises and disappointments. By the time we have a few decades under our belts, most of us live on autopilot, doing what we think we *should* do without looking too hard anymore at what we *want* to do. Our lives seem just fine on the surface, but in the quiet hours we have doubts.

I thought my life would be more meaningful. I thought having kids would make me happier.

I thought I would eventually catch up to the women around me and stop feeling so inadequate.

I thought he would love me the way I long to be loved.

This itch inside us wiggles and twists and tries to wake up. It reveals itself by putting us constantly on edge and making us easily irritated, agitated, aggravated, short-tempered, and reactive. We say and do things we wish we hadn't said or done. Or the tension leaves us nervous, jittery, and anxious, prone to racing thoughts, difficulty sleeping, and discomfort interacting in social situations. And then there are those of us weighed down by long-held grief that leaves us paralyzed, depressed, lethargic, lacking interest or energy.

Bestselling author and research professor Brené Brown wrote an article about her "midlife unraveling" that went viral, mostly because of this powerful observation:

> Midlife is when the universe gently places her hands upon your shoulders, pulls you close, and whispers in your ear:
>
> I'm not screwing around. All of this pretending and performing—these coping mechanisms that you've developed to protect yourself from feeling inadequate and getting hurt—has to go. Your armor is preventing you from growing into your gifts. I understand that you needed these protections when you were small. I understand that you believed your armor could help you secure all of the things you needed to feel worthy and lovable, but you're still searching and you're more lost than ever. Time is growing short. . . . It's time to show up and be seen.[1]

At Selah Freedom, we have a card that we hand out to girls on the street. It says simply, *"Ever wonder if there's more?"* That's a powerful conversation starter, and I've considered carrying those cards around with me in my everyday life as well because the message is true for everyone.

For far too long we've told ourselves that there isn't more, that we don't deserve more. That this mundane, disappointing, fear-filled, suck-it-up life is all we get. But that's just another lie.

My marriage looked great from the outside. My husband ran his family's business, and I stayed at NBC for a couple of years, then left to go to grad school. As a couple, we socialized with the right people and volunteered as leaders in our church.

I never felt fully comfortable in the North Shore, though. I was a first-generation American woman with a wild past, trying to fit into a neighborhood where I was sure I would never belong. I worried about my kids growing up thinking it was normal to be picked up by limos for second-grade birthday parties. "Lord, give them a story," I prayed one day. "Don't let their lives be this vanilla."

In my twenties the messages I'd learned from my parents' marriage affected me deeply. I worried constantly about marrying someone who would set me up for failure. I focused on not falling into some of the most obvious traps I'd witnessed as a child in my conflict-thriving extended family.

But by focusing only on what I wanted to avoid, I let my emotional pendulum swing to the other side, and I ended up marrying someone who was just the opposite. My husband avoided conflict, rarely expressed his emotions, and didn't react even when I was in the wrong. He was happy to let me take the lead in our relationship, which, to me, seemed ideal at first. But anything out of balance can only stay standing for so long.

Have you ever stepped away from the crazy busyness of your to-do list and considered how the messages of your past affected the places where you are today? How were you groomed? What's your story?

Those aren't simple questions, but I believe the answers are already rising inside you. One of the most powerful gifts that every person has is that of discernment—what I learned early on to call that "still, small voice." Discernment helps you intuitively recognize truth. So stop, set aside all the distractions for a few minutes, and really look at your unique story.

Every encounter you had left an impact on your spirit, soul, and mind. How did those affect who you've become?

If that single question seems too big to tackle, here are ways to break it down:

WHAT WAS YOUR CULTURE?

Culture can mean a lot of different things. You might think first about your ethnicity, the country where you or your parents were born, your faith background, or your family's socioeconomic status. Trust your discernment to lead you to the answer that most affected you.

Your culture defined whether you went to synagogue or church, the country club, or an Al-Anon meeting on Sundays. It still affects whether you think of dinner as something to share as a family, eat at your desk, or skip altogether. Your culture influences what you think it means to be a woman, a wife, an employee, and a mother.

You might still live within the culture of your childhood, or you may have left it far behind. No matter how different your life is now, though, the culture you were born into played an important role in how you were groomed, just as my noisy, middle-class Puerto Rican relatives blended with my rural farm family to affect how I eventually felt in the upper-class world of the North Shore.

WHAT WERE THE NEVER VOWS YOUR CULTURE LED YOU TO MAKE?

When I was a young adult, I vowed I would never be dependent on a man for money, and that promise led me into relationships with a host of other problems.

Another woman I know watched her older brother get picked on by bullies at school, so she swore she would *never* become a victim. Today her aggressive, confrontational nature often gets her in trouble in relationships and at work.

When we make vows, we pause and plant flags to mark our identity. If we make those commitments from a pure place, with an eye toward the future, they can lead us in good directions. When my friend Janet vowed to stop drinking, her mental and emotional health improved. When Mother Teresa vowed to dedicate her life to serving the poor, it led her to found the Missionaries of Charity.

But the never vows (*I will never depend on a man for money, I'll never get divorced, I'll never have children who get into that kind of trouble*) are almost always made because we're reacting to the past instead of planning for the future. Our never is connected to something we experienced and reflects our judgment against it rather than our plans for something new.

Never vows are defensive and based on past wounds, and they rarely protect us from the outcomes that we fear. In fact, as has been true most of the time in my own life and in the lives of the people around me, the things we say we'll *never* do come right back to us in one way or another.

To understand the ways you were groomed, you need to acknowledge any never vows you're holding on to. How did they affect your decisions?

WHAT WERE YOUR DEFINING MOMENTS?

As a counselor, I've studied lots of different methods for unpacking a person's past, but I've found the simplest method is often the most effective. You don't need a therapist or any special tools. All you need is a quiet place, a pen and a piece of paper, and some time to reflect.

First, clear time in your schedule. Grab a pen and some paper and go to a quiet place where nothing will interrupt you. Turn off your phone for a while. (The world won't end. I promise.)

Across the top of a blank sheet, label up to six columns, depending on your age now. Mark the first 0–7, the second 8–12, the third 13–17, the fourth 18–34, the fifth 35–49, and the last one 50–present.

Under each column, list the most important events and memories you have from that age range. List both three to five highs and three to five lows—the memories that fill you with joy and the memories that still hurt to think about. Trust your discernment to bring the most important memories to your mind first. If you have a strong memory that doesn't feel like a high or a low, make a note of that too. These moments may not seem significant right away, but you remember them for a reason.

Perhaps the first thing you remember is going to your grandmother's funeral when you were four. Or maybe it's something that happened while you were playing with the neighbors in their tree house. Or it's the day your dad moved out of your house and in with his new girlfriend.

Give yourself time to recall details. What stands out? Is it something someone said? An emotion you felt? Something you saw? Follow your memory as far as it goes. If you were playing in the tree house, what happened next? If your strongest memory from adolescence is the first time a boy kissed you, follow that event as far as you can remember. How did you feel in that moment? How did you feel later?

Don't second-guess yourself, and don't ask anyone else what they remember. These are the life events that are significant to you, and they'll be different from what your friends and family would list or remember. That's okay. Everyone registers and remembers events differently.

When you're done, spend some time with your list. These events groomed you for your future, which is why you still remember them. Winning a spelling bee in sixth grade may have given you the message that you were smart and good with words, which affected your decisions to be on the school paper and eventually become a writer. The close friend who betrayed you in high school and stole your boyfriend, though, set you on a path of never vows that have made you anxious and jealous in your relationships ever since.

When you put your past onto paper, you start to see it in a new way. Patterns emerge, and you start to ask, *What are the pieces I love about my story?* and *What are the pieces that still hurt to think about?*

Okay, here's where my story gets a little weird. Stick with me.

When I was pregnant with my third child, I developed placenta previa, a dangerous medical condition that can cause bleeding and puts both the baby's and the mother's lives at risk.

My doctor ordered full bed rest, but with two toddlers at home, I didn't see how that was possible.

I hadn't told anyone about my condition when a friend called me out of the blue. Renee and I had kids in the same preschool a few years before, but we hadn't spoken in a long time.

The last time I'd talked to Renee, she'd been in a difficult place. A few months before, she'd been diagnosed with a serious kind of cancer, and she confided that the prognosis was dire. While she contemplated her treatment plan, a Catholic priest she'd met through a friend asked if he could talk with her because he had the gift of healing and wanted to help her.

Renee had been understandably skeptical, but she'd asked me for my thoughts because she knew that I came from a Christian background and was deeply involved in my church. I told her she had nothing to lose. She went, and as the priest prayed for her, he put his hand on the place where her tumor was. To her shock and mine, her cancer disappeared completely.

Now Renee was calling again just as my own health was at risk. She was ready to share her experience with a few people, she said, and so she was going to host a "healing mass" at her house with the priest from the hospital. Did I want to come?

Did I? It was a hard question to answer. I'd grown up in a church that believed in the spiritual gift of healing, but that had been in Arkansas, where I'd been molested on the way to church. After that experience I'd rejected every charismatic, Spirit-based teaching I'd learned there. Plus, I had a whole list of problems with the Catholic Church. So why would I want to meet a Catholic priest with the charismatic gift of healing?

I remembered what I'd told Renee. I, too, had nothing to

lose. I wanted to see if this priest's gift would heal me the way it had healed her. But I wasn't convinced, and I asked Renee not to tell him about my condition. This man would need to earn my trust.

The night I went to her home for the healing mass, the priest and his prayer partner took me to a room upstairs, with Renee and another friend as witnesses. He asked what he should pray for, and all I said was "a healthy pregnancy."

He laid his hands on me and started to pray, but I could feel right away that something wasn't right. He stopped. "Something's in the way," he said. "Something is blocking our prayer. It feels as if there's something between you and God." He tried again.

He was quiet for a long minute and then said, "It seems like there's another baby."

He asked if I'd ever had miscarriages. I never had. He tried again to pray. After a series of failed attempts, the tension was rising in the room. And then it hit me.

"Seventeen years ago I had an abortion," I whispered.

"Have you ever confessed it?" he asked.

After debating the fact that I was not Catholic and didn't "do confession," I finally admitted that my abortion had always been a deeply buried secret, one that I rarely acknowledged even to myself.

"Okay," he said gently, not taking offense. "Catholics and Protestants can agree on the need for healing, right? You think you might need some healing?"

I couldn't disagree with that. So the priest started to pray again. He prayed for a long time, sometimes speaking in tongues, while anointing me with oil. Many more things came up over the next hour that I'd never shared with anyone: my secrets of pornography and alcohol abuse and the verbal abuse I'd suffered and, in turn, inflicted on others. As each of my secrets was brought into the light, I felt a new burst of freedom.

The room filled with the smell of incense. And then, I'll never forget, he stopped and said, "It's done. You've been forgiven. You're now as pure as the driven snow. I believe now we can pray about your pregnancy."

By that point I'd forgotten I'd come there with a physical problem.

Once again the priest started to pray, and this time he told me almost immediately that there was something wrong with my placenta. Mortified to have kept this from him, I confessed my diagnosis of placenta previa.

The priest laughed and said, "Well, you've had every other secret taken care of tonight. I think God can take care of this too." And he did. When I went back to my obstetrician the next week, there was no sign of the placenta previa that had threatened my pregnancy.

But that night we still weren't done. The priest whom I'd treated with such suspicion had one more thing to tell me: "I want to give you the gift of tears."

It had been years since I had really cried. When I'd moved to Florida as a teenager, I'd hardened my heart against everything that was hurting me. But that night I wept. I grieved for the last twenty years of living as a lost soul. I grieved who I had become. I grieved what had been stolen and what I had taken from others.

I still don't know exactly how it happened, but when I left that room, I was whole again, with a new level of freedom.

The ways we were groomed can lead us in a lot of directions. Some of them are positive. If you had great, loving, stable parents, chances are they raised you to be a great parent. That part of your life is likely going well. If you had mentors and teachers who encouraged you, taught you, and guided you toward being a strong and compassionate leader and communicator, then you've been well prepared for that part of your life. Early romantic and sexual encounters where you were treated with respect and love created the foundation for long, healthy relationships.

Those "high" memories that you uncovered on your worksheet are things to celebrate and feel thankful for. They're gifts not to be taken lightly.

But no one's life comes without hurts. No one's story comes without something to overcome. And those "lows" also influence you today. Oftentimes they're holding you back. Most people who go through the "highs and lows" exercise find that it's easier to remember the lows and that they remember them in more detail.

Why do we hold on to our pasts so tightly? Why do wounds we suffered decades ago still leave us so shaken? We're smart, capable, and emotionally intelligent. We know, logically, that what happened to us when we were young wasn't our fault and that pain and grief are supposed to go away over time. We realize it all rationally, but emotionally we still have deep feelings of shame, guilt, or pain.

Science tells us that the human brain is wired to remember critical experiences in sharp detail. We form our strongest memories when our brains register high emotions like rage, love, and especially fear. Trauma actually rewires parts of our brains, creating new neural pathways that strengthen our fight-or-flight responses when certain stress hormones are released. And since the brain forms most of its neural pathways during our earliest years of development, the highly emotional memories of our earliest years are burned deeply into its contours.

I didn't fully come to understand how all this works until I met Dr. Jason Quintal, Selah Freedom's national clinical director. He's a key part of our team, and an important part of my personal journey.

"Nobody would care about past experiences if those weren't somehow negatively affecting you now," he says. But to change the now, Dr. Q says we need to go back and identify the critical moment that's blocking us. Remember the "defining moments" exercise earlier in the chapter? This is why it's important. We have to find these critical memories before we can unplug them.

The girls who come through our doors at Selah Freedom all have the deep psychological scars of sexual abuse. They've had countless painful interactions with people, and they haven't been listened to or heard for a long time, if ever. They have a lot of anger and resentment on top of their guilt, and it affects the ways they react to even the most benign situations.

When they come to us, we have a couple of options. We could tell them to forget their pasts and focus on helping them build great futures. Our staff could provide education, resources, safety, and plenty of love. But we know from experience that isn't enough. Unless we stop and help a survivor deal with her past, her refashioned neural pathway connections are always going to be there, bringing repressed feelings of trauma and pain into her life and blocking her from a healthy future.

What's true for the girls at Selah is true for you as well. Those memories of abuse, bullying, neglect, or rejection don't just go away if you ignore them.

When I interviewed him in the process of writing this book, Dr. Q told me, "Let's talk about the forty-year-old who was date-raped as a teenager. She knows that it wasn't her fault and she didn't do anything wrong. So why does she still feel guilt and shame? Why does she still have all the hurt? Because at an emotional level her brain doesn't know that the negative experience is over. That means it doesn't matter that she knows where she's logical. If emotionally her brain still thinks the awful stuff is happening every time an event in her present triggers it, it doesn't matter what she tells herself. She's never going to feel different until the memory is acknowledged and unplugged. Then the emotional charge is gone, and she's not haunted by it anymore. She's not going to be troubled because she doesn't have that emotional reaction anymore."

How do you help someone unplug a trauma? By keeping that person emotionally present when remembering the past, as that priest with the gift of healing did with me.

That priest's prayers kicked off a whole new journey for me. Overnight, the behaviors I'd hidden myself behind disappeared from my life. I never again drank to black out. I was never again tempted by porn.

Growing up in the church, I learned that the key to getting past our human darkness was taking "every thought captive," as the Bible says in 2 Corinthians 10:5. But what I came to realize in my late thirties, as I approached that "unraveling" midlife, was that taking a thought captive didn't mean covering it up or denying its existence.

For years I'd been leading women's groups through my church, using my education in counseling to guide them while hiding myself. After my healing it was time to turn all that knowledge inward and get honest. I was feeling deep emotions for the first time in decades, and I was determined to rediscover the sensitive, loving person I'd once been.

Over the next seven years I did an enormous amount of self-reflection. I read all kinds of books. I went to small groups and retreat centers. I was basically a self-healing junkie. I inventoried my encounters and looked for key memories that still impacted me. Often I discovered places where I needed to ask for forgiveness, and with a lot of work and newfound humility, I rebuilt relationships. Slowly I uncovered the person I really was, pure and peaceful.

But even as I was experiencing this renewal, things at home were crumbling. To ease the financial burden and to relaunch, we sold our house in Chicago and moved to Florida.

It was there that my passion for helping other women deal with past trauma really found its home. I started volunteering as a counselor in a women's center, and that led me to a gathering in 2009, where the seeds of Selah Freedom were planted.

I went from being a woman constantly running from her past to one who embraced it as an opportunity to help others. Without those experiences of loss, abuse, addiction, fear, and shame, I could never have said to the girls who come through Selah Freedom, "I understand. I see you. I believe you. And I'm here to tell you that it will get better."

But my renewal was bittersweet because it came with a cost: my marriage.

I've committed to being totally open and transparent with you in this book, not holding back any secrets, yet it breaks my heart to share this part of my story. I made a solemn never vow when I married my husband: *I will never get divorced*. I'd lived through the damage of that as a child, and I saw the pain it caused my mom. I would weather any challenge or storm rather than put myself or my kids through that.

As I've said, my husband and I were each other's perfect match when we met. Our preferences and soul wounds aligned, and we filled our empty spaces with the same things. But when I started to heal, that fit shifted.

We tried to make it work for years. We sought counseling from professionals and invested in conference after conference. We separated, reconciled, renewed our vows, and separated again.

I had no greater desire than for my marriage to work and for us to stake this new ground together, but that wasn't to be. The divide was too wide to cover anymore. The things that had brought us together now drove us apart. Eventually, after long family talks, the kids and I moved out, and he filed for divorce.

That's not the way the story works for everyone, or even for most women who discover their healing. But that never vow I'd made about divorce, based on the fear I felt from my own childhood in a broken home, came back to bite me.

Are you ready to uncover the lies that have held you back and set out on your own journey of healing?

For most of us the path is a long, slow process of rediscovering an identity of worth and value. We have to gain understanding about how the things that have happened to us are not because of who we were. False messages separated us from our true selves.

It will take time, but the journey begins here and now, with the work you've already done and the work you will do. On the pages that follow, I'm going to explore and describe what I see as five of the most pervasive, common areas of grooming that women today experience. Then we'll spend time talking about what to do with this new knowledge.

Each example of grooming you'll find in part 2 has both a positive and a negative message associated with it. One of my favorite phrases is "No matter how thin the pancake, there are always two sides." That fits here. We might be groomed to be role models, to be supportive, strong, faithful, and generous, but when those positive traits are drowned in negative messages and painful memories, the result is something darker, depleting instead of enriching.

These five examples of grooming aren't based on any scientific surveys, and they're not meant to reflect the experiences of every woman. Not all of these will apply to you, and some of your experiences may not fit into these descriptions. But digging into them will hopefully spark your own questions and help you find words to describe your experiences. They will show you the variety of pathways that women like you can take to let go of the darkness and walk into the light that is freedom.

The first step is to name your grooming.

Part 2

WHAT ARE YOU
GROOMED FOR?

Chapter 4

GROOMED FOR APPEARANCES

*The message you heard: "You exist
only to make me look good."*

W hat am I going to tell my friends?" My father said exactly
what I knew he would.

I was nineteen years old and had announced to my family
that I was leaving Purdue University after just one semester. I'd
gotten my life mostly together by that point and worked hard
at school, but the transition from the sunny beaches and relaxed
attitudes of south Florida to the plaid, preppy, frat-house culture of Purdue was too much for me. I knew I didn't fit in, and
staying wasn't going to change that. I called my dad and told
him that I was coming home to sort myself out and make a
new plan.

"You can't just drop out of a Big Ten school!" he said, and
I knew that what he worried about wasn't *my* future but his
image.

I love my father. We have an amazing relationship today, but it's taken us years to get there and for me to appreciate the positive things he taught me, like how not to be defined by the past when there is an unknown, limitless future in front of us.

My dad moved to Chicago from Puerto Rico when he was fifteen. He spoke no English, but he was charismatic, charming, and determined to realize the American dream. He was the first person in his family to have a white-collar job, and he had great success. His goal was always to reach the highest level of society that he could, so he was always conscious of the image he projected.

It was important to my father that we lived in the best neighborhoods, wore the "right" clothes, and took the best trips we could afford—and, sometimes, couldn't afford. (We'll talk more about that in chapter 8.) Today my dad still dresses well and always has a group of friends and admirers around him. He's truly living the American dream.

Like many men of his generation, my father saw his family as an extension of himself. Whatever my mom, siblings, and I did, it reflected on him. If I wore something he didn't like or said something that embarrassed him, I heard all about it. I learned early that it was better to go along and not rock the boat, but I could be as opinionated and determined as he was. Tempers flared often in my house, and when that happened, all anyone could do was hunker down and hold on tight.

So I wasn't surprised by my father's reaction when I, the first of his children to go to college, told him I was dropping out and coming home without a bigger or better plan. It never occurred to him to ask how the situation made me feel or try to understand where my heart was. Instead, he focused on how a bunch of people I didn't know or care about would see my decision.

I pretended indifference that day. "Tell them whatever you want," I said. But in my heart I experienced the same sinking feeling I always did when I knew I'd disappointed him. He was a powerful force in my life, and as I grew up, I battled constantly with the feeling of falling short. In his world where appearances were all that mattered, it was easy to believe I had let him down, that I wasn't pretty enough, thin enough, smart enough, successful enough. I kept trying harder, pasting on a fake smile and checking my reflection in the mirror one more time to make sure that, despite whatever was happening in my head, everything on the outside looked just right.

I'm not alone in this, and, compared to so many of the women I meet, I had it easy. Many of us—from every part of the world, every race, and every economic background—truly believe we need to act like we have it all together all the time. You know the kind of women I'm talking about. They're moms who excel at work, host Pinterest-worthy parties, and chair amazing fund-raisers. They never seem to lose their cool. Whether they're taking the kids to the playground or dressing for a night on the town, they're beautiful, stylish, and confident. They're always positive, always agreeable. They wear the right clothes and always seem to know what to say and do. Every day they make the world run more smoothly.

I never thought that I was one of "those" women because I compared my insides to their outsides. I would admire them from a distance, sure that those perfect women saw through all of my insecurities and judged the ways I didn't measure up to ideal appearances.

Eventually, though, I had to spend more time in their circles through work, church, and volunteer projects, and I realized something: *those women I thought were so intimidating believed I was one of them.* They looked at the polished surface my father had taught me to show, and they saw something familiar.

I was shocked. Couldn't they see that behind this facade I was busy, flawed, and barely keeping it all together? And then I started to think, *If these women I so admire believe I am one of them, does that mean they're hiding behind appearances too?*

I shared my story with a few of them, and those seemingly perfect women started to share their stories with me. They weren't what I expected. Depression. Anxiety attacks. Panic in response to tiny mistakes or imperfections. And always, always, the deep fear of someone's reaction.

Almost every one of those seemingly perfect women had a powerful, charismatic person in her life or past who held a role like my father's. From those authority figures, they'd all heard, implicitly if not actually out loud, the same message: *your value comes from me, and your purpose is to look good when you reflect me.*

Their intimidating success, grace, and appearance on the surface masked their painful secrets. Because when children hear the message *You do not matter as much as I do* from people they trust, it affects them for the rest of their lives.

When you're groomed for appearances, someone else sets the standards for what is "enough" in your life. Their priorities—whether physical appearance, grades, behavior, or something else—become your priorities.

Women who were groomed for appearances know how to respond to the powerful people in their lives. They know what makes those people happy and what makes them angry. They know when to give in. They know how to look their best. They know which words build an ego and defuse a situation. They respond to other people's expectations before their own needs, every time.

Now that I know what I'm looking for, I can usually recognize a woman groomed for appearances because she loves to talk about what she's doing and about the important people in her life. She's organized and agreeable. But when I try to ask her questions about herself—what she dreams about or what she believes—her messages get tangled. She's never spent much time considering what's happening inside. Her depth of insecurity and fear is well covered but seemingly bottomless.

"It took me forty years to realize that I was always playing a supporting role in my own story," one woman told me.

She'd grown up with a dominating father. He wasn't abusive. He rarely even lost his temper, but that might have been because no one ever contradicted him or tried to argue. He was that kind of man. His house was his castle, his family was under his leadership, and he called the shots. He regularly told his sweet and agreeable wife, "You sit there and look pretty, and I'll take care of everything."

As my friend grew up, he took care of everything for her too. He explained which were the best classes to take and the right extracurricular activities to join, and he guided her toward making certain kinds of friends. My friend was as sweet and agreeable as her mother, and she loved to please her father. She never noticed that no one in her family ever asked her what she wanted, and she never tried to suggest anything that would contradict their desires.

But letting her family dictate the details of her life—she once dumped a serious boyfriend because her father didn't like him—had consequences. Like many women who were groomed to please, she was attracted to men who were strong, decisive leaders. She was an expert at "absorb and reflect" behavior, and it was easy to turn her attention to a man who, like her father, wanted to "take care of everything."

Unlike her father, though, my friend's husband turned out to be emotionally abusive. "I'd never seen someone get angry like that before. No matter what I did, I couldn't help him control his temper." It took years before she gathered the courage and resources to leave him. And even now, after ten years and plenty of therapy, old habits are hard to break.

"When I started dating someone new, I was sure he was different. But is he? Am I? Last week he told me I should get rid of my dog, and I think it's because he doesn't like dogs. That same afternoon I started e-mailing friends about finding Bailey a new home. I never spoke up and said that I didn't want to give up the dog, and he never seemed to care what I thought."

I never recognized how much my own grooming for appearances still affected me until I saw my feelings reflected in someone else's words. I realized I'd been acting the parts I'd been given to make the powerful charismatic figures in my life look good.

Perhaps you, too, feel that reading these descriptions is like looking in a mirror. If you're not sure whether you were groomed for appearances rather than authenticity, here are some questions to ask yourself.

Look at those early memories you identified in chapter 3.

- Was there a dominant personality who insisted you look or act a certain way in public so that you wouldn't cause embarrassment?
- Were you ever shamed by someone you loved or trusted because of something you said, wore, or did?
- Did your family act one way when you were outside the house and another when you were in private? Were there family or personal secrets that everyone explicitly or implicitly agreed to hide?
- Did you ever make a decision about your future and change the direction of your life, or were all your decisions made for you?

Think about the most important person in your life today.

- What do you disagree about? How do you express yourself when you disagree?

- Does this person ask for your opinion or respect you when you express your thoughts?
- Do you use most of your time or energy meeting that person's needs?
- Do you ever cover up or lie about something they have done so that others won't think less of either of you? Do you feel responsible for how the world perceives them?
- Do you ever hold yourself back because you don't want to upset them or create a conflict?

Think about your closest friend.

- If I asked your friend to describe you, what three qualities would come up first?
- Does your friend know what you're struggling with right now?
- Does your friend know the darkest secret of your past?
- In conversation together do you ever cover up your feelings or hide an event, pretending that everything is okay even when it's not?

Think about yourself.

- How much time do you spend in a day worrying about what others think of you?
- Do you make decisions about your appearance, your work, your parenting, or how you spend your free time based on what you want and believe or on what others will think?

- How often do you put on a brave face when you leave your home so no one will know what just happened inside?
- Do you feel like a "bad person" when you make a mistake? How do you feel about yourself when your spouse or child makes a mistake?

⤙

Did those questions tug at your heart? Did you find yourself emotionally nodding a few times too many for comfort? Have you, like so many women, been turning yourself inside out to keep up a certain image while allowing your real self to fade? Even when everything looks great on the surface, do you feel like you're screaming inside?

Let's look at how you got here. Most of the women I've met have been groomed by a parent, but I also know women whose worth and value were subsumed by coaches, grandparents, teachers, siblings, or spiritual leaders. Your groomer might have been a military officer or stay-at-home mother, business leader or Sunday school teacher, immigrant or millionaire. The role itself didn't matter as much as how smoothly they lived it.

From the time you were young, you were taught through words and actions that what you wanted wasn't as important as what your groomer wanted. Your value came not from who you were as an individual but from how you absorbed and reflected that person.

In some cases your affiliation with his power or charisma made you popular or enviable to the outside world. "You're so lucky," people told you, and you did feel lucky to share a popular name or connection, even if you wished that the person you shared it with wasn't so hard on you.

For most of us, our groomers weren't intentionally cruel or abusive. Their own early messages carved their personalities and expectations in certain ways. Perhaps they wore a mask that never slipped. They went through all the right motions without ever missing a beat, and you never saw beneath the surface. You entered adulthood not knowing what real emotions look like.

For some of you, though, the brightness of your groomer's personality turned off behind closed doors, and their need for power and control turned dark. You may have lived through dramatic outbursts and emotional or even physical abuse. I've heard so many stories of growing up with adults who would scream at the breakfast table, berate their children in the car, and then paste on a perfect smile when it was time to go out in public. These became your earliest secrets.

In these cases fear often mixes with a powerful love and admiration for groomers who allowed you to be a small part of their lives. You may have felt an overwhelming need to protect them by never letting anyone see them lose control. "Don't upset things" became your motto, and you learned to be agreeable. Whatever happened in private and whatever you felt, the most important thing was always to put up a good front.

As you grew older, you may have internalized the need for rigid expectations. Maintaining control is something that shows up often in women who intuitively feel they are being controlled. You filled your days with back-to-back activities that drew the admiration of others. You tried to be the star athlete or the student leader. What seemed natural for others always felt out of reach and artificial to you, but you kept it up. You wanted to fit in. You wanted to please.

Or perhaps you labored, and sometimes obsessed, over your looks. Many women who were groomed for appearances focus extra attention on their bodies. You may be hyperconscious of what you wear, what you look like, and how you measure up to others around you. Eating disorders and other secret addictions emerge when this need to control becomes overwhelming.

How did those early messages carry into your adult life?

Time passed, and you grew up. Most women separated themselves, at least physically, from their groomers. Perhaps your shift into the adult world came with blessing and guidance. Or perhaps you're still caught up in your groomer's shadow, still dominated by that person who has never given you a moment of your own in the sun. Or perhaps there was a messy break when you rebelled and declared your independence.

"I don't need you!" you shouted as you slammed the door on your narcissist groomer. You moved out of your parents' stifling house. You quit the job with the domineering boss or left the church where the pastor demanded cultlike obedience.

But a young woman who breaks from a powerful groomer often finds herself flailing, unsure of how to guide her own destiny. When you've been controlled by another person's standards for so long, it's hard to recognize your own opinions and intuition.

Girls who were groomed for appearances often become women who don't know how to look beneath their own surfaces.

They've spent their lives focused only on what shows to the outside world—the way they look, the titles that follow their name, using perfect words in every situation—and don't know who they really are as human beings or what they want.

As a young professional woman, still living by the standards of appearance my father set for me, I would often panic while driving to work. Something was wrong, but I didn't know what it was. I just knew I didn't want anyone to see me like this.

I wasn't ready to face what was in my heart or how my pain was leading me into all sorts of negative behaviors. Instead, I focused on what my outsides looked like. I can't tell you how many times I stopped at Marshall Field's on State Street and bought a new outfit to wrap myself in like it was armor. Surely if I looked this good, no one would notice the real me.

I found my worth in buying clothes I couldn't afford. Others seek the cover of another person. Women who grew up driven by the need to present a good front and not rock the boat often seek out other strong charismatic individuals. It isn't long before a new dominant person takes control of their lives. These women continue the cycle of turning over their emotional needs and self-esteem because that's the only way of life they know.

If you're drawn to narcissists, chances are they're drawn to you. Their radar picks up that you're eager to please, and they see that your carefully cultivated outside makes them look good too.

Eventually you've spent so many years trying to live by other people's standards that you've lost sight of yourself. Who are you if you're not a reflection of someone else?

Don't misunderstand me: You're a strong person on your own, and most people who meet you consider you beautiful, confident, and successful. You're a leader in the community, a go-getter at work or on the PTA. You're always on time, always put together. On the outside you look great.

But what about inside?

↵

Focusing too much on appearances takes all our energy and focuses it on what other people see, leaving nothing left for who we really are.

"It's like I'm coming into a three-ring circus," my dad teased good-naturedly one weekend as he took in the extravagant decorations and over-the-top activities at my child's birthday party. But I knew that he, of all people, appreciated the effort and the appearance. My children couldn't have store-bought cakes or generic decorations from the party store—or, God forbid, a party at a park or other venue.

What would people think?

For ten long, stressful years I lived in this "adult" place of striving to be perfect. I put my energy into what people could see: a great house, expensive clothes, the perfect family. I volunteered in the community and was a role model at church. I hid my true self, whoever she was, deep in the shadows where she wouldn't embarrass anyone. I became the queen of the double life. Day after day I showed up and showed off even when I felt miserable.

When I finally started to break free from the most damaging messages about my identity, my energy to keep up the image started to wane.

I had a nursing baby, two active preschoolers, and a troubled marriage. One morning I realized I just couldn't get out of bed and face another day. In that vulnerable moment one of my mentors happened to call me.

"I can't do it all anymore," I told her in despair.

"Oh, thank God," my friend replied. "Whoever told you that you *should* do it all? Take off your Wonder Woman belt so the rest of us feel better." Her words made me laugh, and I felt some of the tension melt away. Maybe I had misunderstood what everyone else wanted all along. No one expected me to be perfect except me.

What is the cost of being someone who doesn't really know herself?

No one should play a supporting role in her own life. No one should be afraid to speak up, to express an opinion, or to show some vulnerability.

Once you recognize that this desire to please didn't come from inside you, you're ready to awaken to the person you were meant to be. You're ready to allow her voice and empower her desires and goals.

Will it change your current relationships? Probably, but often it's for the better. I've seen dozens of relationships revived and reignited when a partner who has been dormant starts to wake up. When you stop worrying about what things look like and start to speak your truth about the things that matter to you, that can become a catalyst in your marriage, your workplace, and with your family. The people you love and respect will have the opportunity to love and respect you—and you'll all be delighted to get to know the real you.

Chapter 5

GROOMED TO BE INVISIBLE

The message you heard: "Your existence doesn't matter to me."

I cofounded Selah Freedom with two unique and gifted women, Laurie Swink and Misty Stinson. We're as different as three people can be, with our own challenges and our own stories, and our journey hasn't always been easy. But together we accomplished things in those early years that we never could have managed alone. Their friendship and honesty opened my eyes and my heart to how the vastly different ways we were each groomed shaped the women we are today.

Not long ago Laurie's mother passed away, and as she went through her mother's effects, Laurie found a letter her mom had written to a friend. In it her mom had detailed the things she considered to be the highlights of her life: moments from her youth, her marriage, and her long and successful career. Not once did she mention her only child. Laurie didn't make the highlight reel of her mother's memories. Ouch.

The omission stung Laurie's heart, but she wasn't surprised. It was par for the course for the way she'd grown up. Her parents weren't cruel or abusive. They always met her physical needs. But her relationship with them didn't go much deeper than that. They rarely engaged their daughter emotionally.

"I was invisible," Laurie told me. "That was my internal message: *I'm invisible*, so of course they don't pay attention to me. *I'm invisible*, so of course I don't matter in the room right now."

I'm invisible, so I have no value.

Laurie can't remember her mother ever offering her an encouraging word or compliment. When other people said kind things, Laurie's mother would shut them down. Laurie still remembers the day her mother's coworker commented on how pretty Laurie was, and her mother answered, "Yeah, she's okay." When a neighbor jokingly said something about how Laurie would carry her weight as an adult, Laurie's mom relayed the message. "Missy says you'll have a big butt someday," she told her sensitive daughter with a smile. Yet her mom was quick to praise other people, talking with warmth and admiration about coworkers, neighbors, and friends. It was only her daughter who could never earn a kind word.

Laurie grew up believing that she didn't matter to anyone, and so she stopped mattering to herself. She was obedient, never doing anything to get in trouble or draw more negative attention. She shied away from deep friendships or doing anything that would make her stand out or be noticed. She was terrified of speaking to teachers or other adults. *If my own mother believes there's something lacking in me*, Laurie subconsciously reasoned, *it must be true.* She entered adulthood not believing that she deserved anything. Any need felt like a burden that she was imposing on others.

In college, when a kind family invited lonely Laurie to lunch, she lied and said she had homework to do. She couldn't handle the idea that they would do something generous for her. She didn't believe she deserved it.

Over and over Laurie sacrificed herself, doing anything she could to help others. After college she took a job as a teacher in a special education program. She was happy and comfortable in the classroom but dreaded parent-teacher meetings where she'd be forced to interact with her peers.

Her life strategy was to keep her voice quiet and her thoughts to herself. Everyone around her was more important than she was, she believed, because in her heart Laurie doubted that she even existed.

When I first met Laurie, I saw right away that she was gentle and kind to everyone. She was a peacemaker, a personality trait I've never had, and I admired her ability to give so selflessly. But over time I realized that Laurie wasn't just making peace. She was actively avoiding conflict of any kind. She would back down from any conversation that felt like a confrontation or disagreement, and in our early years of working together, my assertive style left her in tears more often than I want to admit.

Laurie is generous, humble, and kind. She always puts others first. Everyone at Selah Freedom knows that Laurie would turn herself inside out to meet any of our needs. But the flip side of all those virtues was that Laurie was living like a martyr, sacrificing her own voice and wisdom when, actually, those very things are what we needed most.

Women like Laurie are in every corner of life though they're not the people you notice at first. They're unsung heroes who stay in the background, working tirelessly but never too close to the spotlight. Unlike the women who were groomed for appearances, they dress, speak, and act in ways to draw as little attention to themselves as possible.

Women groomed to be invisible sacrifice themselves over and over without complaint. They're the ones who can be called on at the last minute to make dozens of cookies for a PTA event. They'll clean up after a fund-raiser and stay up all hours doing their kids' homework and their husband's laundry. They're the women in the office who are given the most work but also the least responsibility or recognition. All too often they're stuck with the blame when anything goes wrong because they never defend themselves.

It's easy for other people to take advantage of women who believe they're invisible because they'll do anything they're asked and never push back. Need a ride to the airport at four in the morning? Need someone to pick up your groceries while they're out shopping for their own? Need someone to watch your kids, proofread your report, serve coffee, or listen to you talk? These women will be there because they derive their sense of worth from what they give rather than who they are.

Don't get me wrong: helping other people is admirable, and not everyone with a servant's heart acts out of a sense of invisibility. But far too many women hover in the background because they believe this unhealthy message: *You're here to serve, not to be recognized. You don't deserve anything more.*

That last sentence shifts everything.

The women who were groomed to be invisible will do almost anything to avoid conflict, real or imagined. They'll never ask for a raise, a promotion, or recognition of any kind—and often if public recognition is offered, they'll reject or run away from it. It doesn't occur to them to stand up for themselves, and if someone else expresses anger, they're the first to apologize. I know a woman who was so intimidated to talk to strangers that calling for pizza delivery gave her panic attacks.

Their friends call them givers, but behind their backs people whisper the word *doormat*. They're walked all over in every corner of their lives. And they'll never utter a peep of protest because who would hear them? They're invisible.

You've read enough about my life by now to know that this doesn't describe me. But I've always been surrounded by women who felt invisible, starting with my mother. She's beautiful, but for a lot of reasons—her lack of education, her troubled marriage, and probably whatever messages she heard when she was a child—she was never comfortable in the spotlight. As my father's personality grew and his reach expanded, hers shrank.

Have you ever explored the five love languages first described by Gary Chapman in his book of the same title?[1] My mom shows her love through acts of service. She's never been physically affectionate or verbally affirming, but like many women who were raised to give, she does things for those she loves all day long. Even in my most rebellious, hard-hearted years, I could always depend on my mom for a backrub, clean laundry, and dinner on the table.

My mom taught me how to receive, but as I look back, I'm not sure anyone was giving to her in return. She lived for years on the emotional outskirts of our noisy family's affection, attention, resources, and acknowledgment—not because we didn't love her, but because often it was hard to see her. She hid herself away, remaining quiet and distant even from her children.

Over the years I saw resentment start to take root. She complained more and smiled less. Still, she almost never told anyone no. Like most conflict avoiders, her anger leaked out in more passive-aggressive ways.

Do these descriptions sound familiar? If so, this chapter might be hard to read because it shines a light on your inner self, and that's not something you often face. After all, if no one else notices you, why should you spend time getting to know yourself?

Women who are true, healthy peacemakers are some of the strongest, most life-giving people I know. Breaking free from the unhealthy messages we were groomed to believe creates space where you can be truly and fully known by those who love you—the whole you.

To get there, we need to find the places where your grooming has gotten in the way.

Look at those early memories you identified in chapter 3.

- Are there examples of someone showing you love and acknowledgment? Are there places where you felt rejected, ignored, or unloved?
- How often do you remember feeling alone or unnoticed?
- Did anyone ever give you the message *I wish you'd never been born*, either explicitly or implicitly?
- Did the people closest to you build you up in front of others and help you develop your unique strengths?
- Did you have someone in your life who was your advocate when things went wrong? Was there someone you could go to who would empathize with your pain?

Think about the people closest to you (your partner, family, friends, or colleagues).

- Are you comfortable offering them your opinions about decisions, events, or ideas, even if those opinions contradict someone else's?
- Do the people closest to you ever ask what you think? If so, do they really listen to your answers?
- What was the most recent kind thing someone offered to do for you? How did you respond?
- Have the people close to you ever blamed you for something that wasn't your fault? Did you defend yourself, or did you accept responsibility?

- Do the people close to you praise you in public? If so, how do you respond? If not, how does that make you feel?

Think about yourself.

- How do you show love to your friends and family?
- What is an issue that you care deeply about? When was the last time you spoke up to advocate for or defend it?
- Do you find yourself doing favors for people even when you don't want to?
- How do you express your anger or frustration?

If you see yourself in the stories or in the questions above, there's probably some part of you that has been trapped by the feeling that you're unloved or unwanted. You were groomed to believe that you don't matter. No one ever helped you see the unique value you brought to the world.

How does a message like that start?

Perhaps you were caught between strong personalities who were often in high-volume conflict, and your invisibility was a defense mechanism. You hid to survive your parents' tumultuous marriage, life with a violent or unstable person, or traumatic events happening in the wider world around you. You convinced yourself, *If no one sees me, no one can hurt me.*

Some of you were told flat-out, "I wish you were never born." Others didn't hear those words but felt that same message. You believed that your very existence made things worse, or at least harder, for people you loved. You saw the financial pressure that caring for you put on your young, single mother. You felt like a burden in a family with too many children and not enough space.

If I didn't exist, their lives would be better.

Maybe you were groomed for invisibility by adults who never attacked or criticized you but who were simply too caught up in themselves to notice the needs of anyone else. If you tried to express yourself, your feelings were dismissed or minimized. Often our groomers are too wounded themselves to understand the consequences of their actions.

Since no one sees me anyway, I must not exist.

Whatever happened, no one acted as your advocate. Your pain was yours to bear alone. Accepting help or kindness felt unnatural and undeserved, even as your heart cried out for love and encouragement.

Since no one was listening, you never developed a voice, and each time you were ignored, rejected, overlooked, or belittled, you sank deeper into the story that your voice didn't matter anyway. The less you shared yourself, the more the fear of sharing overwhelmed you. You navigated adolescence without making waves, terrified of being called on or called out.

But human beings need to be noticed, and you longed for true relationships. If no one would notice you for who you were, you determined that they would notice you for what you did. You became a helper, always available for anyone and ready to fill the holes left by everyone else.

"Not belonging is a terrible feeling," wrote author Phoebe Stone in *The Romeo and Juliet Code*. "It feels awkward and it hurts, as if you were wearing someone else's shoes."[2]

If no one has ever come along to draw you out of your shell and show you how much you matter, those early messages might still affect how you live today. For most women the results are stifling but not dangerous.

It's easy to spend all your time meeting the needs of others. You earn your place in the world by constantly being agreeable and subservient. You avoid the spotlight—any spotlight—at all costs. If you never learned how to receive love or kindness from others, you may now have trouble accepting genuine respect or attention from others. When someone reaches out, you flail defensively or push back, and everyone ends up feeling awkward.

Your friends and family know that you're the dependable one, the reliable one, the one who will be there for anything, no questions asked. Most of the time they take you for granted—not because they are trying to hurt you but because they can't respect your boundaries if you've never established any. If you seem happy, or at least content, doing all the housework, running all the errands, and working the hardest shifts, why wouldn't they leave that for you? Why would they invite you to parties if you've never shown any interest in being included? Why would they ask your opinion if you've never expressed one?

Just as you are groomed to give, many others have been groomed to take. Until they find out how much is happening inside you—how much wisdom you're holding back from sharing with the world—they don't know what they're missing. They'll suck you dry because they can.

Of course, there are also narcissists and even sociopaths in the world who seek out and prey on people they consider doormats. They see an invisible victim sign flashing, inviting them to swoop in and take over another person's life. In the most dangerous of cases, girls with low perceptions of their own sense of worth and identity get caught up in a predatory pimp's web. When faced with the pressure to sell themselves, they aren't prepared to put up a fight.

Living as a person who believes she's invisible is suffocating, limiting, and ultimately destructive.

Over time the pressures of living for other people start to build, and many women find themselves filling with resentment. They're deeply hurt by those who dismiss them even though they never actively seek attention. But the answer isn't to put blame on others and keep hiding. The solution is to take charge of your own story, let go of those early grooming messages, and uncover your unique, valuable voice.

For Laurie, the turning point of her life came when she cofounded Selah Freedom. She had hidden herself for more than forty years, avoiding conversations or situations where her deep wisdom would be obvious and valuable, but when she heard the shocking numbers and heartbreaking stories of sex trafficking victims, something broke open inside her. She became more passionate about helping girls who'd lost much of their self-esteem than she was afraid of stepping up and stepping out.

Laurie's deep concern for supporting survivors pushed her into risky places, but she made it clear to everyone that she didn't want any "on stage" roles in the organization. She didn't see herself as a spokesperson or a leader. That wasn't working for any of us. Laurie was—and is—the heart and soul of Selah Freedom. We needed her deep understanding of the values and culture that formed our foundation. We needed her expertise in education and curriculum development. Most of all we needed her to believe in herself so that the fragile girls coming through our doors would also believe in her.

Misty and I begged Laurie to speak up in meetings and in front of the community. We were relentless in our pursuit to show the world—and Laurie—how important her gifts were.

The girls loved her. The board and staff of Selah committed to her. And a group of close friends prayed her through the tough process of confronting her past. It was only when Laurie saw how deeply she'd wished for her parents' acknowledgment and how much her mother's words affected her that she could separate their treatment from who she really is. The threat of rejection passed, slowly, from her, as she realized that her perspective was valuable in the conversations we were having.

For every woman I know who lives with the message of invisibility, the path to healing begins with learning how to say no. When you create boundaries and set limits for who you want to be, the real you—honest, strong, unique, and loved—shines through. When you value yourself, you encourage other people to value you.

One day Laurie and I were talking through a decision related to Selah. I was engaged and dramatic, rapidly firing off my ideas and waving my arms around because I *really* wanted her to agree with me. In the past these conversations had ended quickly, with me pushing and Laurie retreating like a turtle into her shell. She'd agree with whatever I said, whether she believed me or not. But that day Laurie held her ground. She didn't retreat, she didn't cry, and after twenty minutes she still didn't agree with me. I was the one who finally said, "Okay, we'll just have to agree to disagree here."

It was the first time she'd ever stood up to me about anything. It was one of the first times she'd ever stood up to anyone about anything. And it was wonderful.

Today Laurie is one of the healthiest women I know, full of quiet confidence and unconditional love. We can call on her at the last minute to speak to a group of four or forty, and she's there. She brings all of herself to every meeting, party, and conversation.

One of the things we offer to the girls in the Selah Freedom safe houses is college preparation, an important step on the path to a new life far from the streets and cameras. When Laurie first started taking Selah Freedom girls to visit campuses, she noticed that almost every one of them would freeze.

I don't belong here. Everyone else here fits, but I don't. The underlying messages of invisibility and doubt were there, and even as the girls accepted their roles as survivors, there were places they couldn't see themselves going. They didn't recognize their leadership abilities.

Because of her own experiences, Laurie knew that she

would never be able to talk the girls through college if their internal message was that they didn't belong. Instead, she decided to show them the potential she saw in them. She developed a program to try something new—a leadership training program that is now part of the national Selah Freedom curriculum. Every girl who enters the program is assigned to facilitate a group; together they read a book or explore a topic. For most of the girls, the experience is eye opening. "I never expected to be in front of other people," we often hear. "I never thought that I could lead anything."

Now, thanks to Laurie's insights, when the girls visit college campuses, they're more prepared. They can see themselves participating in discussions with their peers, speaking up, and offering opinions.

They no longer feel invisible and can see themselves as the strong, necessary, and loved people they are.

Chapter 6

GROOMED TO ENDURE

The message you heard: "You're stronger than everyone else. You can handle it all."

When I think about my marriage, I think about the two Saint Bernard puppies we brought home one night. My husband was a dog person. I was not. I already had three kids to raise. But he insisted that he would take care of our fluffy additions, and I believed him.

We carried the two thirty-pound behemoth puppies into the house. A few minutes later, he announced that he didn't feel well and was going to bed.

"Don't worry," I said as he headed for the stairs. "I've got it. I can set up their kennels and figure out what to do with them." And no, I wasn't being sarcastic. I thought I was being strong and supportive. I thought spending three hours wrestling with dog supplies by myself was what I needed to do as a good wife.

That conversation sums up far more of our relationship than I understood at the time—not just about my ex-husband's coping methods and carefree attitude but about my own responses.

When we first met, I thought I'd finally found a grown-up. He was older than me, with a stable family business and financial security. For years I'd been the grown-up and the giver in my relationships. I was always willing to carry the people I loved. *Now I'm finally going to be able to rest and have balance*, I thought. *He'll take care of me.*

But, instead, I continued to be the caretaker. I was independent and assertive, used to filling the gaps of other people's emotional and physical needs. Before long I was managing finances, kids, the house, parts of his business, my volunteer work, and our social calendar.

"It's no problem," I'd say when yet another project, like those dogs, fell into my lap. When the leaders at church or the school PTA needed someone to take on yet another role or spearhead a new committee, their answer was, "You want it done well, give it to Elizabeth. She can handle it."

When our finances started to shift and I couldn't afford to pay for the help I needed to manage our house and family, I rolled with the same mantra.

"I've got it," I'd assure my friends.

I was efficient, organized, capable, and oh so tired. Trying to do it all—raise my kids, save my marriage, and rediscover myself—was depleting. But I never let anyone see how exhausted I really was. I kept leading groups, signing up for programs, and going to marriage conferences. I was convinced that I could power through anything.

The only thing I couldn't do was admit defeat. I'd made too

many of those internal never vows, and, like I said, the strongest one was *I'll never get divorced.*

"I don't care what's going on," I told one of my friends not long after I started Selah Freedom. My personal life was in free fall, but I couldn't admit it. "I believe anything can be restored. We save girls from sex trafficking, so surely I can save my marriage. If I can help a girl who was left for dead in a garbage bag and watch her become a thriving and fantastic person, then I've got this. My marriage is having a rough season, but we're pushing through. It will be fine."

My friend let me talk, but when I finally wound down, she gave me a look and asked the question I dreaded. "Are you really okay with all this?"

For a long time—probably too long—I *was* okay with it. I was driven by pride, convinced that there was nothing I couldn't fix, nothing I couldn't endure. Other women might struggle or give up, but I was stronger than that. After all, look how far I'd come. Look at what I'd already overcome. Every relationship had issues. I could handle this. I would not let myself fail.

But my friends didn't give up. "I'm going to send you a book," one said. The book she gave me was about troubled relationships, and the quotes and examples described my situation to a T. I recognized myself on almost every page, and I realized with a sinking heart that I'd normalized textbook levels of dysfunction. I already understood that my earliest messages and experiences—my grooming—had desensitized me to a certain level of dysfunction, but now, no matter what I'd told myself about how things would be okay, my eyes were opened.

That was the first time in my life that I wondered if enduring was really what I wanted.

↢

This powerful urge to endure whatever comes my way is at the heart of who I am. It's been groomed into me over years of experiences, and I know I'm not alone.

It's easy to recognize other women who endure rather than live fully. They're the ones who keep all their plates spinning even though their eyes are tired and their smiles seem pasted on. They talk about how much work they have to do, how little sleep they're getting, and how busy they always are. They share that they're juggling tough bosses, troubled kids, demanding volunteer work, needy husbands, aging parents, and busy social calendars without ever asking for help. At times it feels like a competition. *Oh, you're going through that? Well, let me tell you about my challenges.*

They're the "stable" people in families that are full of need and conflict. They put up with things no one should have to endure.

A woman once confessed to me that her husband could become abusive when he drank. She would hide in the pantry after her children went to sleep, waiting for him to pass out. She'd even sleep there, setting an alarm for the early hours of the morning when she could safely sneak into her own bed. When her children woke up and came to find her, she'd paste on a cheerful face and ask, "Who wants pancakes?" Then the day would begin, business as usual.

She was proud of herself for keeping her family together, and it took years for her to see the cost to her own heart and soul.

Unlike women who are caught in the trap of appearances, women who endure don't try to hide the craziness of their lives from their friends and peers. They want people to know how much they're juggling. It's what gives them a feeling of value and place in the world. Women whose lives are stripped down to only what they show on the outside feel a lack of self-worth, but women who are groomed to endure are sure of their own inner strength. It's everyone else who is weak or wanting.

Some see themselves as role models, and they use their challenges as opportunities to show everyone else how much a person can do. They lead book clubs, committees, and women's groups where they tell other people how to live even as they turn a blind eye to the mounting piles of mess in their own lives. Like me, over and over, they assure everyone, "I can handle it."

They've been holding things together for as long as they can remember, and they don't know any other way to live. There's never been a time or place for them to have needs of their own, so they push away introspection. If a friend asks that powerful *Are you okay with this?* question, they'll do what I did, and say yes.

Remember how I told you that people tend to tell me their secrets? Part of the reason is because I radiate the I-can-handle-it vibe. My whole life I've been both a fixer of people and a collector of people. Women groomed to endure are attracted to broken people, and broken people are attracted to us. They confide in us because we seem strong enough to carry their secrets.

When children are groomed to be caretakers, they learn that the whole world needs them to fill that role. If they let go or give up or admit that there are things they can't handle, everything they care about might fall apart. Like me, most people who endure instead of living have always been surrounded by needy people. Over and over they heard the message *I need you.* And they believed it.

That deep fear of collapse drives many of us to become uncomfortably controlling, demanding that everything run according to our agenda. Unlike the women who were groomed to be invisible, we don't hesitate to step in and confront someone whose ideas or agendas don't match our own. Enduring women tend to be leaders, not doormats. We are convinced of our own strength. We don't trust others.

But there's something missing. I can recognize the women whose lives are driven by a message of endurance because behind their competent, confident, and often prideful exterior, there's no joy. Life is only a series of struggles to overcome and problems to solve.

Does any of this feel familiar to you? Are you reading this book in snatches, between checking off items on your long lists and responding to interruptions from the many people who depend on you? Here are some questions to help you find out if you were groomed for endurance at the cost of your own inner peace and future.

Look at those early memories you identified in chapter 3.

- Did you grow up in the shadow of someone who needed you to care for them?
- Was there a traumatic or painful event, or series of events,

that dramatically changed your life and shifted your family's attention?
- Did you ever feel like you were the caretaker, either physically or emotionally, of the adults around you?
- Did the people who influenced your early years believe that their role—and therefore yours—was to meet the needs of others?

Think about the people closest to you.

- Has someone listened to you share how things are going and asked, "Are you okay with that?"
- Do the people in your inner circle all depend on you to meet their physical and emotional needs?
- If one of your closest friends was living with the challenges you're currently dealing with, what would you advise her to do?

Think about yourself.

- When something painful or difficult happens, how do you respond? Do you keep plugging forward, managing the everyday aspects of life as if you weren't just rocked by an earth-shattering event?
- When was the last time you felt a true, deep emotion like joy or grief? How did you express it?
- Who do you depend on when you need emotional support or help? Is there anyone you trust to take care of you?

- Have you ever taken a full day or more away from everyone you know in order to focus on meeting your own needs? What did that look like?
- Do you ever wish that someone else would step in and take over, at least for a little while? Have you ever asked someone for help?
- How do you respond when someone asks you how you're doing?

As I said, the grooming messages of endurance tend to start early. If you see yourself in the descriptions and questions above, you probably grew up surrounded and deeply influenced by some kind of need, whether it was someone close to you with physical or emotional needs or your whole family was rocked by trauma or conflict.

Family dynamics change radically, for example, when a member develops a serious illness. The center of attention shifts, and even children find themselves feeling the pressure of providing physical or emotional support. This is even truer when the illness is mental rather than physical.

Writer Laura Zera grew up with a single mother who suffered from psychosis. "As my sole guardian, my mother was the most important person in my life. And under her roof, I played by her rules, no matter how bizarre, because losing her was unthinkable," she wrote in a *New York Times* essay. "In the midst of the maelstrom, I'd reached an unconscious yet uncompromising conclusion: my mother's behavior was my problem to shoulder, and I shouldn't expect anything different."

As a child, Laura shielded her mother, never telling anyone when she was forced to brush her teeth with Comet or had to listen to verbal abuse about the color of her eyebrows or the position of her arms. Laura endured, eventually moving out of her mother's house. But the scars remained. "Like the tidy, studious child I was, I front as an organized, high-functioning adult. I must persevere to move through the world without falling down."[1]

You might have been groomed the way Laura was, or you may have grown up in the shadow of a world-rocking accident. My outlook on myself, the world, and my place in it always comes back to Diana.

I have a specific memory from those painful months after my sister's death. I was running down the stairs, and my brother—the same brother whose gun had accidentally discharged—had hidden at the bottom. He jumped out to scare me, something he'd done a hundred times before. I was always easily startled, and probably more so at that sensitive time. I startled and screamed, and then I got mad.

"Stop it! I hate you!" I shouted at him. And then the clincher: "I wish you would have died instead of Diana."

I was a kid, and the words flew thoughtlessly out of my mouth in that house where no one ever said her name, aimed at a person who had his own reasons for feeling her death deeply.

I'll never forget the way he looked at me in that moment. It was like I killed him. *What I had said*, I knew instantly, *was the worst thing in the world.*

Not long after that, my brother left to join the navy, and

I didn't see him for years. My young mind, already groomed by the suffering around me, internalized the message that my words and actions had destroyed a person. My seven-year-old heart believed that I had sent my brother away. For years after that, I carried the subconscious message that I had an incredible power to destroy others if I spoke. So I buried my truth deep inside and learned to endure heartbreak in silence.

The survivors who find their way to Selah Freedom have endured shocking things. From their earliest abuse to the violence and humiliation of life on the streets, they've "handled" things that most of us can't even imagine. A lot of them end up in this place of endurance, becoming the caretakers of everyone they meet, even their pimps. They hide their own experiences behind a tall, thick wall of bluster and deflection. "I can handle it," they say, even as they go back to sex work.

Perhaps your story isn't so dramatic, but it still began in a place where you were the one meeting needs rather than having them met. You might have been the oldest child of many, always on call as an extra set of hands. Or you were the child of social workers, missionaries, pastors, or other community servants who gave themselves selflessly to those outside your home, grooming their children to also prioritize the needs of others above their own. You always had a sense that at any moment things could collapse, and the people you loved would suffer. You felt that it was up to you not to let things fall apart.

Whatever your story is, you came to this place of endurance through hard work and a genuine desire to help others. You have an incredible gift of strength, and it has served you and the community around you for years. But if it has left you feeling like your entire purpose in life is to "keep it all together" and be the tough one, the strong one, then you're missing something.

⸙

Today you have everything and everyone around you under control, but there's a giant gap in your soul where you've buried your own vulnerability and honesty. You were groomed to believe that you exist to care for others, but that's left you without space to allow your own needs to be met.

You may surround yourself with people who want or need to be cared for, and the cycle continues. You continue to feel like the only stable person in a world of instability, and there's no one to trust but yourself.

That early message you heard—that the people you care about always need you to give and never receive—has left you exhausted, depleted, and emotionally isolated. Your vague awareness that you're barely holding yourself together pushes you to do more, be more, and control more.

Your work is mostly thankless. Instead of expressing gratitude, your loved ones push back against the self-protection that might come across as coldness or pride. You've been accused of being distant, bossy, or unapproachable. Those broken, needy people in your life are caught up in their own messages and issues. You hold it together as they belittle you, berate you, and refuse to acknowledge the almost heroic effort you're putting in. And yet you stay.

You stay because, with everything that's going on, you don't have room left to feel anyway. You understand that enduring isn't living, but what choice do you have? The world couldn't handle you starting to let go, even a little bit, of what's building up inside. And, like me, you may have made one of those never vows that keeps you bound to an uncomfortable, unhealthy, or downright dangerous situation.

When you live in a place of false pride, believing that you're the only one who can hold things together, you sacrifice trust. You don't mind sharing your dramatic stories, but only on your terms, as examples of how much you can handle. Vulnerability is probably a dangerous concept for you because it means opening yourself up to input, not just sympathy. There's no place for anyone to get close to you, to see and support the person you *really* are.

Do you even know who that person is? Who are you, as a unique and complex human being? Who are you when you're not the protector and defender of others? Have you ever given yourself permission to stop, to be still and quiet and alone, and find out?

Until we reach that breaking point, nothing ever changes.

Human beings need both to give and receive. When we're groomed to endure, we learn how to give over and over again but never to receive in return. The hole in our hearts keeps growing, and eventually something has to give.

For some people that comes after years of silent resentment. *Don't they see how much I'm doing for them? Why doesn't anyone ever give as much as I do?*

For most others, though, it comes with exhaustion. We just can't do everything for everyone anymore. As we start to peel back the layers of our own false narratives and see how unhealthy our relationships have become, we do something radical.

We carve out space for ourselves.

After I read that book my friend gave me about dysfunctional relationships, I started to pull back. I realized, finally, that I couldn't keep trying to fix or cover over everything, especially as conflicts rose faster than I could choose to ignore or overlook.

So I moved out. I started to live the principles I'd tried to teach others, including the girls at Selah, for years. It was not my responsibility to fix anyone, and another person's wounds were not reflections of who I was. For the first time in my marriage, I created lines that I would not allow to be crossed.

Dr. Henry Cloud and Dr. John Townsend tell a story in their bestselling book *Boundaries* about a time when a couple made an appointment with Dr. Townsend for their adult son, who was going through a number of problems. On the day of the appointment, the couple arrived without the son. They said that he didn't want to come. "He doesn't think he has a problem."

"Maybe he's right," Townsend said. "Tell me about it."

The parents told him about their son, who had problems with drugs and hadn't been able to stay in school or hold down a job. They'd bailed him out time and time again.

Dr. Townsend let them talk for a while. Finally he told them, "I think your son is right. He doesn't have a problem. . . . You do. He can do pretty much whatever he wants, no problem. You pay, you fret, you worry, you plan, you exert energy to keep him going. He doesn't have a problem because you have taken it from him. Those things *should* be his problem, but as it now stands, they are yours. . . . As it stands now, he is *irresponsible and happy*, and you are *responsible and miserable*."[2]

When we are groomed to believe that the world depends on us to endure, we often see the faults and weaknesses of others as our problems to solve. But they're not. No matter how strong we are and how capable, we can't make other people less needy. We can only enable them to focus their needs on us.

Remember, the people who groomed us are often not bad people, and neither are the adults who engage with us as the people we were groomed to be. My ex-husband is not a bad person. He was groomed just as much as I was, and his wounds matched mine for a long time. When I started to break free from the unhealthy messages of my past, we didn't match anymore. Now he has his own journey, and removing myself from it was possibly the best thing that could have happened to help him move forward. It gave us both the opportunity to get to better places apart than we could have together.

But my story is not every woman's story. Far more often the women I meet who are rediscovering how to hear their own voices and carve out spaces to be their true selves experience deeper relationships. For example, I have a friend who spent the first twenty years of her marriage trying to be the emotional rock—always calm, always giving, always anticipating everyone else's needs. She took pride in the fact that she'd never cried in front of her husband. But that stoic front was hard for him to see through. He didn't understand the real her, and their marriage had cooled into a polite distance.

Then, at a family wedding, my friend uncovered a repressed memory of abuse that shook her to her core. For the first time in her life, she couldn't just plow past a situation. Suddenly she couldn't stop crying. My friend's husband responded to her vulnerability with layer upon layer of compassion. He started to see his wife in a new way, and the two of them have gone on to build a beautiful relationship of mutual giving and receiving.

Women who were once groomed to endure can learn to carry generosity, strength, and compassion into new places in life where they can thrive as whole people. But on top of that, they can discover a new level of vulnerability.

We can learn to let go and to trust. Our relationships become stronger as we open ourselves to people who love us and allow them to give as well as receive. Our joy deepens as we unpeel our fingers from the tight control we've been holding. And as we let our past go, our future opens to new stories we can't yet imagine.

Chapter 7

GROOMED FOR JUDGMENT

The message you heard:
"You are unforgivable."

Not too long ago one of the survivors living at a Selah Freedom safe home—let's call her Allison—shared her story with me. She'd grown up as a good kid with loving parents who took her to church every Sunday and dropped her off at youth Bible study every week. When she turned thirteen, Allison noticed that the Bible study leader started singling her out and paying extra attention to her, and it made her feel special. But then one evening, when they were alone, he touched her inappropriately. He apologized and told her not to tell anyone. He could lose his job in ministry, he said. But then it happened again and then again.

Allison kept her secret for years as the youth leader's sexual abuse continued. He would assault her, then blame her for "tempting" him and demand that they both pray for God's forgiveness. Later she would have to sit silently as he led youth group discussions about sexual purity.

Filled with shame at what she considered to be her guilt in allowing this to happen, Allison never told anyone. Her secret took a toll on her heart. She grew depressed. Her grades fell. She started getting in trouble at school. Allison's parents, confused by the change in their daughter's behavior, encouraged her to get more involved with church, where the Bible study leader continued to use and abuse her.

When she couldn't take it anymore, Allison ran away. It was better for her to disappear, she thought, than for her parents to find out what she'd done. She imagined their anger if they realized that she'd given up her virginity and how the whole church would judge her. She didn't tell anyone that she was leaving, so there was no one to help her find a shelter or place to stay. Instead, Allison got on a bus and rode it as far as it would take her, trying to physically put her past behind her. She arrived in a city she'd never seen in the wee hours of the morning. Less than twenty-four hours after she left home, Allison was approached by a pimp who was staking out the bus station and must have seen her desperation from a mile away. Her Bible study leader had already groomed her to be easily coerced and controlled, and the pimp had sixteen-year-old Allison turning tricks in less than a week. Eventually she stopped praying for forgiveness.

When a person like Allison's secrets and hurts overlap with the spiritual messages and values she's held for years, the consequences are often devastating. I know this from personal experience.

I told you earlier that when I was in middle school, my friends used to tease me about being such a church girl. I'll never forget us sitting around my kitchen table talking about sex. Who would be the first of us to *do it*?

"We know it won't be Liz," someone said, and everyone laughed. My position as the "good girl" and "church girl" was well known. God said not to have sex outside of marriage. I heard it in my evangelical church all the time, and it had become a core part of my values and beliefs.

Then I went to Arkansas and was molested, and my foundation cracked. Then my parents divorced, and I went to that fateful frat party.

When I looked in the mirror after that, I saw failure. Becoming sexually active—even though it wasn't my idea or my fault—meant that I had failed not only myself and my family but God. My church and youth group leaders talked about sex as if it was the worst thing a young, unmarried person could do. What did God think of me now?

It was one thing to feel like I'd make a mistake, even a big one. It was something else to feel as though I'd failed God. That thought haunted me and drove me into ever-darker places for years as I tried to cover the shame.

For both better and worse, churches and faith communities are among the strongest groomers in many of our lives, second only to parents and immediate family members. Faced with the potential judgment of not only other people but also the Creator of the universe, the messages children learn about right and wrong carry extra power.

In many cases—probably in most cases—those messages are

beneficial, and the influence of a church or other faith community is incredibly positive. Study after study shows that church brings people joy, contentment, and a sense of well-being as they are groomed to serve a loving God, accept forgiveness, and serve others. I can't argue with that.

But remember what I said about there being two sides to every pancake? For all the good that the church does and the truth it conveys, it can also become the place where women end up broken down by imperfect human judgments.

I was at a church-sponsored conference not long ago to speak about Selah Freedom. As I watched the speakers who took the stage before me, I was struck by how each woman presented herself as a role-model Christian, with a perfect family and a perfect spiritual life. The program built up to a woman who, according to her introduction, would be very vulnerable and very brave in sharing the darkest corners of her life. *Finally*, I thought. *It's about time we started getting real here.*

The woman took the stage and through tears described how she, too, had been a perfect Christian wife and mom. She and her husband had raised their kids to obey Jesus and go to church. But something had gone terribly wrong, she said, because (and she really had to struggle to get these words out) her adult son was now *living with a woman he wasn't married to.* That had been an enormous blow to her, and she explained it was a huge step for her to admit this shameful secret to the audience.

I don't want to criticize that woman because this was something she struggled with, and it takes courage for anyone to get up in front of a room and admit the parts of their story that still hurt. But at the same time her talk made me feel uncomfortable. Her confession wasn't about herself or the challenges or mistakes she'd made in her own life. If this church was only prepared for people to talk about that kind of secondhand struggle, I realized my personal baggage wasn't welcome there. My lay-it-all-out-there honesty didn't belong in that room.

These were people groomed for judgment.

Have you ever met a person who seems to live in a box of spiritual clichés? She has a quick answer and a verse for any situation. *Love the sinner, hate the sin! All things work together for good!* When she talks about her faith, she spends most of her time explaining the things she knows she *can't* do or what everyone else *shouldn't* do. She has a strict set of rules for who can't have sex, who can't speak up or lead a meeting, how not to fail in marriage, what not to give your children, and what not to do or wear or say or feel in church. In her mind, God is waiting to smite, reject, and evict anyone who steps outside the boxes assigned to us.

These are the messages brought by people she trusts most: her spiritual leaders. They might be local pastors or TV celebrities, famous authors or social media stars. However they communicate, they've taught her to be loyal to their advice. Her purpose in life, she believes, is to serve the God they bring to her.

According to these all-too-human teachings, some mistakes are worse than others. And if that leaves her believing she's less worthy of God's blessings than someone else or less capable of leadership or that men must be forgiven when they abuse the women who tempt them, it must be true. It's God's will, her teachers assure her, and she clings to that certainty. If God hates divorce or homosexuality or women who have abortions, then the people who turn to these things she'll cut out of her life.

A woman groomed for judgment assures you that there's

freedom to be found in so many rules and security in a God who is hard on anyone who steps out of line. She portrays a kind of holy perfection, sanctified and subservient. And her intentions are good. She desires to live a faithful, holy life and to honor her core beliefs. But she's been groomed to see the world as "us" and "them," and she likes to be part of the "us."

She eyes other women with suspicion, always looking for sin or difference to call out. If another woman's dress is too tight, her hemline too short, her legs too tanned, or her ideas too forcefully presented, she's one of *them* and must be avoided. The women who judge mask their gossip as prayer requests (*Please add Betty to your prayer list because she seems to be having a hard time right now.*), but their voices are sharp and uncompromising (*Well, she just needs to pray harder. God can heal anything.*).

If you listen long enough, though, there's often an underlying tension in this woman's story. Because just as God judges others, he also might judge her if she slips—and we all slip eventually. She worries about any perceived disobedience in her life and hides her grief when the strict bounds of her dogma trap her in situations that don't feel very holy.

She avoids talking about parts of her own story when she's in certain communities because she knows the people there will treat her differently if they know everything. They'll see how much she's failed.

When life gets messy, her desire to obey and earn God's favor bumps up against her church's strong and divisive messages. *Will God still hate my divorce if my marriage is abusive? Would he have given me this passion for teaching if he didn't want me to use it? Can I still have a relationship with my fallen brother or my atheist neighbor?*

How does her love for God line up with her compassion for his people?

She may double down on her rules, believing she is worthy of God's love only if she is obedient to his commands. Obedience is the primary sign of her groomers' messages, after all, so she digs into living out the letter of the laws that were taught to her, and she redirects the judgment she feels until it's once again aimed at others. If *they*'re not living the way *she* believes they should, then it may be up to her to change them. Or at least to express her concerns.

So many people judge because they feel judged, living by the rules even though they secretly know that the rules don't fit their experiences anymore.

And then there are those who just reject it all.

From what I've seen, a person who was groomed with judgment often goes one of two ways. The first is to follow the groomers' example and try to fit into narrow, black-and-white boxes of obedience. The other is to rebel completely.

Our churches and faith communities are places where we should feel safe, where leaders should be honest and trustworthy, and community should be built on love. But humans everywhere are flawed and imperfect, bringing their own wounds and messages into their relationships. So, sometimes, the most traumatizing messages of our early years come from churches.[1]

I've met dozens of girls at Selah Freedom who are angry at the God who allowed terrible things to happen to them. Why did he turn a blind eye to their pain? I understand their feelings. When the worship leader of my Arkansas family's church abused me, I refused to go back to that church ever again, and I turned away from many of its doctrines and teachings for years.

And then there's my friend Jenn, who still wants nothing to do with anything related to God or church. When she was young, her parents took her to church all the time. But when her father abandoned the family and her mother divorced him, Jenn saw the women at church turn against them. They shunned Jenn's mother for committing the "sin" of divorce. They gossiped. In her mom's most vulnerable and wounded place, the church had abandoned her too, and her daughter never forgot. She dedicated her life to staying as far away from faith communities as she could.

Angry at the grooming messages that left them feeling like they didn't matter at all, or that they mattered less or deserved less than others, thousands of women like Jenn have lashed out and rejected their faith altogether.

Yet there's a paradox here: These people are following their grooming to distrust, to reject, and to deny. Still driven by deeply embedded judgment, they invest in fighting all the good that comes from a faith-based community. Rather than embracing the message "It's God's will," they reject it absolutely. They not only leave their human groomers, the ones who hurt them and filled them with shame; they also cut out God in the process.

And can you blame them? We've been swamped with stories of church and ministry leaders behaving badly, using their reputations as servants of God to inflict personal harm. Studies say that 30 to 40 percent of American pastors today have a physical or emotional affair with someone in their congregation.[2] It seems we can't go a month without another high-profile church leader, teacher, or Christian author stepping aside in disgrace, leaving only a trail of betrayal. Turns out it's easier to preach about purity than it is to live it.

The most painful messages of judgment, from what I've seen, don't come from the people involved in a relationship. They come from outside voices, often well-meaning, who rip out whatever ground we might have found to stand on and survive.

In 2018, I saw the viral video of Paige Patterson, then president of Southwestern Baptist Theological Seminary in Fort Worth, Texas, bragging from the pulpit about what he'd told a woman who came to him for help from her physically abusive husband. Patterson said that he advised her to go home to her husband, commit to her marriage, and pray. A while later she came back with two black eyes. Patterson told his congregation: "She said: 'I hope you're happy.' And I said, 'Yes . . . I'm very happy,'" because he reported that her husband, perhaps feeling guilty for his assault, had come to church for the first time that day.[3]

The video made me remember the time a woman came to me and said that her pastor had advised her to stay in a toxic relationship, where she and her children were regularly beaten because "God hates divorce."

"You know what else God hates?" I said. "Abuse."

In too many faith-based communities, divorce is still stigmatized and judged. Well-meaning pastors and church leaders focus on the value and importance of marriage, the hard work that's involved in keeping one healthy. They pound home the message that God hates divorce while never acknowledging the hurting people in their audience for whom marriage isn't only hard but also dangerous.

I stayed in my marriage for many long, painful years after I knew it was over because I'd internalized the message that God hates divorce. Divorce, in my mind, wasn't a last resort. It wasn't a resort at all. It would be another way that I'd failed not only my family but God too.

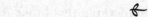

Well-meaning churches and leaders across the country are getting carried away with their own messages, setting themselves up as human arbiters of what God does and doesn't want and what he can and can't forgive.

Trapped in the middle are women trying to live faithfully. Are you one of them?

The faith of our childhood continues to sustain and guide many of us, but if it goes unexamined, it can start to feel constrictive rather than supportive. It's wise to step back and consider what you believe and why. Don't be afraid to ask tough questions about those early messages, even the ones that involve the Creator of the universe.

Look at those early memories you identified in chapter 3.

- Did you grow up in a community with strong moral codes based on faith or religion? Who was the most influential voice in that community?

- Were you significantly hurt by someone you identified as a leader in a faith community? Did you ever witness someone being hurt by people who claimed to represent God? How did that affect you?
- Did anyone ever try to discourage you from a behavior by saying that it would make God unhappy with or disappointed in you? How did you respond?
- Were there social "lines in the sand" that your family or church drew to separate them from others? Was anyone shunned for doing something that broke religious rules?
- Did anyone ever tell you that your gifts were less valuable or that your options were limited because of your gender, race, or beliefs?

Think about the people closest to you.

- Does everyone in your inner circle of trusted friends and family share your faith?
- Have you ever held back from sharing an opinion or experience because you worried that it would be considered out of line?
- How do you respond when someone you care about faces a difficult decision? Do you talk about it together? Do you share what you think God wants?
- Have you ever felt punished for your actions by a church or faith community?

Think about yourself.

- What do you believe God sees when he looks at you?
- Have you held back from doing or saying something because you're concerned about how you will be judged by your church or faith community?
- When you think of God, do you associate him with a particular group of "holy" people? Do you try to incorporate their beliefs into your own?
- Are you currently making painful choices based on what you believe God wants you to do?

If you see yourself in this chapter, probably at some point a trusted parent, pastor, teacher, or other person you respected explained to you what was and was not acceptable to please God. If you were young, your mind was particularly attuned to a fear of punishment and a desire to please.

You grew up hearing pastors and parents tell you what God wants for your life. *God hates divorce. God requires submission. God demands modesty. God expects you to give more than you have. God wants you to shun those who don't agree. God doesn't want you to speak up or lead. God wants you to try harder.* The faith community, which you know should be a safe place, taught you to be strict instead of loving, obedient above all.

Your groomers promised you eternal life in exchange for obedience here on earth, and that sounded like a good deal.

However painful obedience might seem, the long-term benefit couldn't be matched.

They gave you lists of Bible verses to learn and taught you how to apply them to any situation. They assured you that you were special, among the few who really understood the right ways to live. And they taught you fear. Fear of your community's disapproval. Fear of being a bad example. And, especially, fear of disappointing God.

What they didn't tell you, though, was that they are as human as you are and just as likely to fall short of an ideal. Some pastors, Bible study leaders, and even popular authors get used to being treated as if they have something between special wisdom and divine authority. They may have believed that they had special revelation when they taught you about God—the ultimate giver and taker of life, judge of good and bad—and also about morality, modern living, and cultural responses.

Trusting those grooming messages, you let go of God and let other people dictate your conscience. They set your boundaries and taught you how to act. They convinced you that you were worthy of God's love only if you obeyed God's commands—as interpreted by them.

But, wow, there are so many of these commands, and so many ways that things can go wrong.

When life shifts beyond our control, that black-and-white grooming can take a beating. When someone you trust abuses you or your husband leaves or the police call in the middle of the night with bad news or your kids rebel or your best friend tells you she's gay, those Bible verses that always seemed so clear don't cover all your questions anymore.

For a long time, you cry. You pray harder. You make more never vows about not giving up and not compromising and not abandoning the people you love.

All that judgment you once directed at women who didn't seem as strong as you starts to feel false. There was a time when you said, "She just needs to trust God." But now that it's you in the situation, the answers aren't so clear.

When the awe and fear we feel for God starts to thaw, the thing that's been hiding under that perfectly polished surface starts to come out. It's anger, maybe even rage, that others have been working through for years already. *How could God put us into these situations?*

I used to rage at God. All I could see was that he took my sister, then brought a series of men to take my body. I lost my family, my virginity, my friends, and my dignity, all before high school. How was that fair?

How could God take that loved one from me? How could he ask me to endure in a marriage that's so miserable? Why would he allow my family member to make such a terrible choice? Why did he give me this desire, or that obstacle?

All too often, though, expressing anger or doubt at church isn't safe, so we bury it. We judge others more harshly to cover the ways we feel about ourselves. Still, those easy-to-quote Bible verses ring false. Those church leaders have reputations that are a little tarnished in the light of day.

True healing doesn't come from following rules. It comes from honesty and awareness. It comes from spending time listening in prayer, not just talking. It comes from understanding that you are no more or less holy than anyone else, and that we all have a lot to learn. We're all broken in our own ways, and God loves us all anyway.

You see, the truly dangerous message that your groomer gave you was that God would judge you. That God was the one laying out the strict rules, or that failing to live up to any of them could separate you from God.

That's a false understanding of who God is.

God didn't put this fear of judgment in your heart. People did.

I'm not encouraging you to turn your back on your church, your faith, or the God who loves you. Nor am I saying that you need to reconcile with a particular branch of faith that hurt you. What I'm saying is that it's time to separate those false messages of your groomers from the truth of how God speaks to your heart.

God, after all, offers grace. His Son Jesus is a radical forgiver.

So what if, instead of fearing God, we chose to trust him? To take a hard look at how our adult selves understand and practice those early messages? To listen to his still, small voice? What if we stopped judging those who don't live the way we do and stopped judging ourselves for not living up to someone else's standards?

What if you separated your relationship with someone who claims to represent God from your own personal relationship with God?

What if we took our consciences back from our groomers and took a hard look at their motives in guiding us? What if we started to see ourselves with equal voices and equal connection to God?

Wonderful, authentic people who are deeply connected to God don't all see things the same way. They don't all follow the same rules of worship or look at social issues the same way. No single person, church, or denomination represents the full community of faith.

When we separate our deepest spiritual beliefs and connection to God from our grooming messages, we discover a God who is distinct from legalism. We open our potential to living fully as the people we were created to be.

When I held myself back in fear and anger, I couldn't bring together all the pieces of my story, let alone use them to help others. It was only when I let go of the messages that groomed me for judgment—the ones that said I had to keep fighting for a lost-cause marriage, made me suspicious of people in certain churches or with certain backgrounds, and made me present a "perfect Christian" face instead of an honest and authentic one—that I became ready to move into a life of truth.

That path is open to you as well.

Chapter 8

GROOMED FOR FINANCIAL FEAR

The message you heard: "There's not enough for you."

Have you ever had to abandon a full cart of groceries in Costco because you realized there wasn't enough money left in your bank account to cover them? Have you ever needed to apply for scholarships so your kids could stay in school or ask the bank for yet another extension on your mortgage payment? I've done it all. I've lived with extreme abundance and humiliating scarcity.

In the final tumultuous years of my marriage, when we were flailing and the money was flowing out of our accounts, I wondered how I had gotten to this place. After all, I'd sworn that I would never depend on anyone else for money. (Another one of those never vows.)

My early messages about money had left a lasting impact. My parents married when my mom was only seventeen—before she'd had a chance to finish high school. Theirs was a traditional marriage when I was growing up. He was the sole breadwinner, and she stayed home and managed the house. They both had strengths in those separate areas.

My father, very conscious of his image as was mentioned earlier, controlled the way our money was spent. There always seemed to be enough to buy the things he considered important, but there was rarely anything left over. After my parents divorced, things got harder. My dad was still part of my life, but he soon had a new wife to support in a new state. Without a degree, my mom's income potential was limited, and she struggled financially. She had the most beautiful and authentic work ethic, and I've always admired her, but I also realized there was no way I wanted to live like that as an adult.

My decisions as a young adult were bound up in money and how much of it I could make. I gave up my dream of being a broadcast journalist when a mentor explained that I could make more in sales. I worked hard all through my twenties and earned a great income, and at twenty-six I was the youngest person in my family to become a homeowner.

When I met the man who would become my husband, I was financially independent, self-sufficient, and living the life I had been groomed for. I loved that I had my own place, Bulls season tickets, and a nice wardrobe, and I enjoyed showing off all the accolades due to my successful position in the advertising world.

When we started a family, though, I made a risky choice. I left my high-pressure, high-income job and became a stay-at-home mom because that's what women did in our North Shore environment.

Even as I embraced the new life, determined to pour my

time into my family and trust the outcome, I was torn. I wanted to be the fabulous stay-at-home mom that my own mother had been, but walking away from my six-figure income contradicted the never vows I'd lived with for so long, and that left me confused and anxious. The message *You're going from being an asset to a liability* kept resounding through my mind. After a lifetime of measuring the security in money, I found myself in a vulnerable position.

Is it safe to trust someone else to care for my material needs? Am I being stupid, repeating the mistakes I think my mother made? Am I less valuable as a person if I don't have a giant net worth of my own?

I went to grad school for a master's degree in psychology so I'd have the skills for a new career if I ever wanted one, but I focused on volunteering and never took a salary from the counseling work I did in Chicago. The messages I got from my community were that women in our position didn't work for pay. We had a different kind of status.

My grooming for appearances pushed me to keep up that image even when our business struggled and our bank accounts started to dry up, but the fear of running out kept me awake at night. My husband and I kept spending what we didn't have. Looking back, I can see how much we were filling our soul wounds with material goods we couldn't afford, pretending nothing had changed.

Everything, though, was changing.

A quarter of Americans, across all socioeconomic backgrounds, say that money is the thing they think about most on a daily basis—more than family or even sex.[1] And they're not just thinking about it. They're worrying about it. They worry about being in debt, how they'll pay their bills, and what other people will think about their house, car, and clothes.

Their lives are consumed with questions about money. Do they have enough? Will they have enough in the future? What if it disappears? What if other people judge them for not appearing to have enough or for having too much?

They're living out messages that all come down to some version of *Your worth is tied to what you make, what you have, and what you spend, and it's never enough.*

I recognize the women who were groomed for this trap by the way money seems to sneak into every conversation we have. Maybe she's the person who fills her social media feeds with pictures of her extravagant outings, wardrobe, and house. She'll whip out a credit card for "retail therapy" or to donate generously to charities. She may not admit it, but it often looks like she chose her friends and even her spouse based on their net worth and living standards.

Or maybe she's the other side of the pancake, the person who complains about the things she can't afford. She gets visibly jealous of those who have nicer, newer, better stuff. She mentally compares her material life to others' and only feels superior to those who have less. Life is a game with winners and losers, and the person with the most stuff wins.

That's because somewhere along the line she was groomed to believe that what she owns is a reflection of her worth and what she deserves.

Many of the women I've met are living beyond their means, much like I was. They have big credit card balances and late mortgage payments. The debt may be crippling their relationships, but they can't seem to say no because underneath all of the big houses and brand names is a current of fear. No matter how full or empty their actual bank accounts are, they're living on the edge of a knife because they've been groomed to believe that what they have now might all disappear someday.

Girls in Selah Freedom who were groomed to see the world through a material lens have a hard time leaving a life of porn or prostitution because of what they believe it will bring them. Most girls are lured into the sex trade slowly. At first they confuse love for survival sex because they hear the words we all long to hear: *You're beautiful. I love you. It'll be okay. Just trust me. This won't be forever.* When those promises don't pan out, they stay in the life because they're blinded by the attention they get in strip clubs or the gifts their pimps provide.

One of the most heartbreaking stories I've ever heard was from the survivor who told me about running away when she was eleven after being molested for years by her father and brothers. A stranger approached her as she was walking down the street and offered her ten dollars for sex. Her first thought was, *This is great; he's not my dad, and now I can buy McDonald's.*

Girls sell themselves over and over because the tiny bit of security tied to money is the only way they can define their own worth.

There's a lot of overlap between women in a lifestyle of prostitution and those who are groomed for appearances. The messages they receive are aspirational and push these women to create false images for others to admire, perhaps as a way to distract from who they really are under the surface. Women groomed for appearances are constantly measuring what is "enough." They worry that who they are and what they have are never going to measure up.

On the flip side are those women who claim not to be interested in material things at all. Their attention, they assure you, is on more spiritual or practical things. "Managing money and stuff is okay for other people," they say, "but I'm not the kind of person who needs a new car or fancy clothes." They wear their thrift like a Girl Scout badge of honor, defining themselves by simple lifestyles, aging cars, and the great deals they got on the clearance rack. They work hard, but it's not for the money. They'll seek promotions but never a raise.

Beneath their words is an uncertain identity. They, too, link their worth with what they have, but the difference is that they don't see themselves as deserving of nice things. Like the women groomed for invisibility, they push away surface-level desires and settle for whatever anyone offers them.

For both types of women—the materialistic and the thrifty— their sense of self fluctuates with how they perceive their material position, and their identity is wrapped in what's often called a poverty mind-set. They were groomed to feel poor, less than, and inadequate, and they believe there's nothing they can do to change their circumstances.

According to author Donna Partow, a poverty mind-set "puts us in the role of helpless victim. It tempts us to sit back as spectators to our own destiny. We believe everything that happens to us is the result of outside forces. We have no control."[2]

What's important to see here is that when we talk about a

poverty mind-set, we're not talking about how much money a woman has at her disposal. A person can live under the burden of poverty whether she has millions of dollars or is just scraping by. That's because these grooming messages aren't tied to dollars. They're tied to fear and a sense of worth.

When we founded Selah Freedom, our vision was extravagant. My cofounders and I dreamed of enormous, elaborate, gorgeous safe houses spread across the country. We wanted well-paid, caring, professional staff. We aspired to make a real difference in a crisis that was growing out of control.

That all came to pass. Generous donors supported our vision and provided amazing homes and furniture. Brilliant and dedicated employees filled our programs. We grew faster than anyone expected, and thousands of girls have had the chance to rebuild their lives.

The ironic thing is that all of this happened despite the fact that all three of us cofounders were struggling against deeply ingrained messages of poverty and worthiness in our personal lives. For two years none of us took a salary from the organization, even as the accounts showed a surplus and our responsibilities grew into more-than-full-time jobs. "I don't want it to seem like we're doing this for the wrong reasons," I told one of my mentors. Those North Shore messages demanding that women volunteer themselves for good causes and ask for little in return were still strong.

We were creating something that could change the world, but we still couldn't see our own positions of worth in the equation.

We all needed the money. Those were the same years as my aborted Costco trips. Each cofounder faced challenges that would have been helped if we'd been willing to do what our donors and friends all told us to do: accept compensation for our efforts. But we were all women who had learned, through our own grooming and personal experiences, to expect to live with less.

Talking about money and service in the same sentences made us uncomfortable, and it was only when real need overpowered our resistance that we agreed to minimal salaries. Every year after, when it was time for the board of directors to review our performance and recommend raises, we'd question, *What do we deserve? What are we worth?*

Those are hard questions for me to answer even today. I'm still working to get out from under layers and layers of grooming.

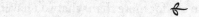

What about you? Are there places in your life where a mindset of poverty and fear is affecting your decisions and holding you back?

Look at those early memories you identified in chapter 3.

- Are there key moments in your past that revolve around conflicts related to money?
- What primary message did you hear about money when you were growing up? Was wealth seen as a goal or something evil to avoid?

- Did you ever have to worry about not having enough to meet your basic needs?
- Were you ever ashamed by not having as much as, or having more than, someone else near you?
- Was there a strong figure in your life who controlled your finances in a way that left you feeling insecure or uncomfortable? Did that person ever withhold money or resources that you needed?

Think about the people closest to you.

- When you describe your family, closest friends, or colleagues, do you focus on what they own, what they wear, or what they spend?
- If you have a career or job, have you ever asked for a raise? What does it feel like to ask for more than what you have?
- Is your family struggling under the weight of debt? How do you talk about that or work to address it?
- Have you ever cut off a friend or relationship because the other person's financial situation was different from yours?

Think about yourself.

- Are you content with your material situation?
- If your financial situation changed dramatically tomorrow (either you lost a significant amount of your income or it doubled overnight), how would that change the way you see yourself?

The fear of finances almost always grows out of our earliest messages and memories.

Money is one of the primary areas of conflict in relationships, and your desire to avoid any discussion or focus on money may have started when you heard your parents repeatedly fighting about who spent what. If one parent controlled all the financial decisions while the other had to go without, you saw how money could be manipulated to control.

You may have heard "We can't afford it" whenever you gathered the courage to ask for something you wanted. A family I know often used the favorite line: "What do you think our name is, Rockefeller?"

Perhaps you also heard resentment. "That's for rich people, not us," Stacey remembers her mother saying over and over, whether it was about joining a community sports team or taking a family vacation. She wasn't sure whether to resent the rich people or feel sorry for herself.

You might have had parents who struggled daily to make ends meet. They were always uncertain about whether you would have food the next day or whether you'd have a place to live next month. That kind of financial insecurity leaves deep scars. It's hard to plan for the future when even basic needs are not guaranteed.

Mary was raised by a single mother, abandoned by Mary's father before Mary was even born. Her mom didn't have much formal education and worked behind a cash register for Mary's whole childhood in order to keep food on the table. "I don't care if you ever get married or have a family," her mom used to tell her; "just make sure you have an education and a career that can support you when it all goes away." Mary has lived in fear ever since of how she will support herself when everything comes crashing down, as she's been groomed to believe it will.

Or perhaps you grew up in a family that spent lavishly, beyond their means. There were piles of presents under the Christmas tree, but also piles of past-due bills on the desk. The stress of debt always hung over your family. Short-tempered parents were often absent, working long hours to provide material goods. You lacked for nothing except time with the people you loved.

For some, money was a forbidden topic, devalued and hidden. To talk about money was crass—even sinful. Desiring a new toy, a new outfit, or college tuition put you on a path of disappointing or upsetting people you cared about.

Time and again you heard, "There's never enough." Not enough money. Not enough time. Not enough for you.

Whether the messages that groomed you were set in a life of abundance or absence, you were left without a feeling of peace or security. You learned that it was dangerous to desire more than what you had because you would be disappointed over and over.

That insecurity probably made you a strong, resourceful person. You started babysitting or working early to make your own money and take care of yourself. Not being a financial burden on anyone was important to you. But no matter what you earned, it was never enough to fill the hole that fear carved on your heart. You've spent your whole life holding your breath, waiting for something terrible to happen.

If you've never faced down those early messages about what you own, they're probably still a part of you, no matter how stable your outside life appears to be. "We become what we think about all day long," said poet Ralph Waldo Emerson.[3]

You brought your concerns about having enough into adulthood, and now they consume you. They may have influenced your choice of spouse, job, and home. They leave you constantly on edge, a little part of you always waiting for everything to fall apart.

If you have financial security, you're constantly aware of it. You may have escaped physical poverty, but not the mind-set. You rely on your bank accounts to cover your soul wounds and try to buy your way to happiness. But that probably leaves you feeling like an imposter because the hole in your heart can't be filled with the right clothes or the best vacation.

Somewhere, deep down, you still think, *I don't deserve this.*

If your financial situation is precarious, or could become so, your day-to-day life is caught up with deep fears for survival. You make do with less, you compromise, and, mostly, you worry.

Deep in your heart, you think, *This is all I deserve.*

Because, again, a poverty mind-set isn't about how much money you have. It's about how you see yourself. It's about what you believe you're worth, and you were groomed by family, friends, or circumstance to think you weren't worth as much as others. You've either accepted that or hidden from it, but you haven't rejected the message. It continues to affect you. That fear that what you have won't be enough follows you, sabotaging everything from your rest to your relationships. It creates conflict in your marriage, sends mixed messages to your kids, and makes your future seem uncertain. It pushes you into careers that don't fulfill you and then holds you back from seeking recognition and compensation in them.

It leaves you in a life of constant fear.

You are more than the total in your bank account, and the same is true for the people around you.

Like I said, this is an area I've struggled with greatly over the years. I still can get highly reactive to any potential financial change in my life, and I'm still unraveling all the messages about money that I acquired from my two very different parents, my community, my jobs, and my marriage. But I'm learning, and here's what I can tell you:

Your life is moving forward, not backward. What happened in your past—the unstable times, the shame, the loss, the uncertainty—isn't coming back. This world you now live in is not a place of scarcity; that was a false message. It's a place of abundance. There is plenty for you, and you deserve to share and enjoy it.

Your worth is not determined by the size of your house, your family, your credit card bill, or your bank account. Whatever happens, you are worthy of spiritual and emotional abundance, generosity, stability, and most of all, contentment.

Contentment isn't the same as happiness, which is a fleeting emotion. Being content is about being at peace in your soul. It's not about settling for less than you deserve. It's about letting go of comparisons with others who have more or less than you and being satisfied with what you have right now, whatever that is, because you're satisfied with yourself.

If a poverty mind-set is a response to life based on fear, then contentment is a response based on fulfillment. It banishes the past and the future from our reactions and opens us to the gifts that are right here in the present.

When you open yourself to a new way of living, you realize we are living in a world of abundance.

Part 3

LEAVING THE LIFE

Chapter 9

SELAH

S top.
No, really. Stop. Whatever you think of what you've read so far—whether you're nodding along and seeing yourself in the stories, you're feeling unsure, or you're positive that none of this is about you—stop.

Before we go further, you need to give it all time to sink in.

When a girl first arrives at Selah Freedom, she's in a vulnerable position. She may have come to us on her own after meeting us at one of the outreach programs we do in courtrooms, jails, or on the street. Or she may have been dropped off by the police or ordered into our program by a judge.

How she arrives isn't as important as what she does with the opportunity once she gets here. The next big step is up to her. Is she ready to "leave the life" and start over?

The question is not as simple as it may sound. These girls—young women, really—have often been on the streets for years. It's a hard, painful life, but it's the only one they know. The traffickers who abuse them are the only people they think they can trust. For years they've been told that sex is all they're good for and all they're worth. They've been bullied, beaten, abused, coerced, and manipulated, and they have lived without any control over their own lives or bodies. It's difficult for them to imagine that they can change.

With all of that over their heads, leaving the life isn't something they can decide one minute and jump into the next. The bonds that tie them to their pasts, and the influence of the abuse they've suffered for so long, go too deep for that.

So at Selah Freedom we have what's called an assessment house, where the girls stay for the first four to six weeks when they come to us. This isn't a chance for us to assess them. It's a chance for them to assess themselves, to stop and be still—something most of them haven't done for years—while they contemplate their next move. This, we tell them, is their *selah*, a word we borrowed from Hebrew that means to pause, rest, and reflect.

We ask a lot of questions during those weeks, and we provide discussion groups, books, and staff members ready to talk, but the ultimate choice is up to each girl. What does she want? What is she able to commit to? Is she ready to let go of everything in her past? Is she ready to dig deep and do the emotionally hard work of changing her life?

Our primary message to every girl in Selah Freedom's assessment house is that she is worthy of being able to see her life clearly and set her own direction. If she's going to overcome her past and move into a healthier, happier future, she must give herself permission to change. She must believe she's worth the effort. Without that internalization, nothing we can do for her will make a difference.

When a girl at Selah Freedom decides that, yes, she's ready, then she helps create a personal action plan for her future. She will eventually move into one of our residential houses, where she'll live in a family-style community full of intense programming for an additional one to three years. There we can help her get counseling with Dr. Q to clear her trauma and reset the neural pathways in her brain. We can help her build life skills. We can help her get medical care. We can help her get her GED and prepare for her next step: college for some, the workplace for others. Basically, we can help her do whatever she needs to make a new start.

But the choice is hers, and it starts with a selah.

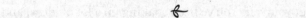

See where I'm going with this?

You have a choice too. You picked up this book for a reason. Maybe it was because your soul was crying out for answers. Maybe you already knew you had unresolved issues in your past and were looking for a way to uncover them. Maybe you simply liked the cover. And maybe you started reading in order to tear this message apart; your primary goal is resistance, not change.

Now here you are, over two-thirds of the way through. I've put a lot of new ideas in front of you and a lot of questions about who you really are and why. Perhaps you see the ways you were groomed. Perhaps you're still not sure.

Either way, before you can go forward without the secrets and messages of your past controlling you, you need to stop.

You need a selah.

The Psalms are a collection of lyrics to songs, and every time the author calls for a musical interlude, the text says, "Selah." *Don't plow through the song*, the psalmist whispers. *Pause so the words sink into your soul.*

This idea of stopping to let all that you've learned sink into your soul might be hard, especially if you're a take-charge, quick-decision woman. You might already be ready with a reaction to what I've said. *Oh my gosh, I see myself in chapter 6! I have to start fixing that RIGHT NOW!* And you might be right. But, please, before you jump ahead, stop. Give yourself time to listen to that still, small voice inside, the one that shows you the truth about yourself. You've been soaking up a lot of ideas, and there might be more here than you see right away.

A selah is also a chance to keep you from running away. *Oh my gosh, this is great content! It's so deep. And now I'm going to put it down and go walk the dog and make dinner for the kids, and I'll push all these hard questions out of my mind and not change anything.* You know in your heart that there's something you could dig into, but you're unsure if you are ready for the consequences. So you add another volunteer job or pull another pint of ice cream out of the freezer, and you distract yourself.

I am the queen of procrastination in situations like this. I'll sit down and crack open a book, read a sentence, think, *Oh, this is going to be so good! I need to hear this,* and then two seconds later, I pop up to make myself some tea or check my e-mail. My kids joke that I need blinders on the sides of my face, like a horse.

Please don't run away so fast. I know you're busy, but nothing in your life will change unless you give yourself time to pause, rest, and reflect. You're here for a reason.

Why did I pick this up? What question was I asking?

Am I jealous of someone?

Do I wonder why my husband and I don't have sex anymore?

Why do I feel resentful of my parents as they start to age and need me more?

Why don't I feel connected in my church anymore?

Why am I always so angry at my kids?

How does what I've read so far help me see these questions differently?

Am I satisfied with the life I'm living?

Am I ready for something new?

There are no right or wrong answers here, so don't strive to think too hard about what you think you're *supposed to* focus on. Take a break from the noisy, always-on world and sit in the quiet. Turn over again and again the questions I've asked. Look at things upside down and challenge yourself to think about them differently. The answers will eventually come.

I don't know what your answers are. I haven't seen your early memories or heard what secrets you're carrying. I can't tell you what your specific next step is after this. But I know that you're looking for something, and your heart is opening to something. Your soul is longing to get unstuck from something. Giving yourself a selah is your opportunity to find out what those somethings are. It's the chance to take my stories, and the ideas I've given you, and make them personal. It's the place where you can identify your own fears, address them, and overcome them.

If you give yourself the time to look at the things you know and what you've been taught, what you've read will sink in and take root, and you'll find your own epiphany. It might not happen today, but if you give yourself time to pause, you'll set the process in motion.

And what you'll find will be fascinating.

If that idea is still too hard to accept, it's okay. Many of the girls who come to Selah Freedom don't stay in the assessment house the first time they arrive. We've learned it takes seven to eight interventions, on average, before a person who has suffered abuse is ready to go down a different road and receive help. Half the girls who enter Selah Freedom leave after a week or two even if they are thriving in the program. In fact, some of the them who seem most committed and excited are the ones who leave first. They come to us and say, "I'm ready to go. I've learned everything I need here, and I'm so grateful." Most of them return to their old lives. Many of them think they're in love with their abuser, or they're sure that they can help their trafficker change. Abuse is all they've known, and even when it hurts, it's hard to walk away.

But if something is stirring in you, it's not going to let go until you face it. You may think you're reading so that you can help your sister because this book is so clearly about her issues. You may think you're not ready now. You may be worried about what your epiphanies will do to your family, your marriage, your friends, or your community. But once a nagging feeling starts, it doesn't stop.

You'll be reminded of it every time you turn on the TV or watch Netflix. You'll see it in your children's behavior. You'll hear it in what you say, and what you choose not to say, to your closest friends.

Eventually you will reach a point where you can no longer pretend that everything's okay. I see it in the Selah Freedom girls, and I see it in the other moms sitting with me in the bleachers while we watch our kids play football. There's a breaking point for all of us, when the thing that we've been trying so hard to avoid talking about comes pouring out. Secrets don't stay hidden forever.

So if you can, stay. Pause and let go of the idea that this conversation we're having is about anyone else but you. If you need to blow off this book right now, I understand. If your place in these ideas hasn't clicked yet, feel free to put it on the shelf for now. Then, when you're ready to think about real change in your life, pick it up again and start with a selah.

What does a selah look like?

On the practical side, it looks like creating a quiet space for yourself outside your normal routine.

I've started going on two-day selah retreats whenever I have a major decision to make, when I feel a transition coming, or when it seems like there's something inside me that's blocking my growth or ability to hear. I know that it's time to pause when my brain starts to feel like the inside of a blender and all my thoughts jumble together. I only get clarity when I'm quiet, and as you've probably picked up, I'm rarely quiet.

Going away overnight isn't always easy to arrange with three kids, a full life, and a fast-growing organization to lead. But getting physically away to a dedicated retreat center, hotel, or even the house of a friend who's out of town can make a huge difference in how much I'm able to turn off the outside world and let my mind wander over the things that need attention.

If getting away for multiple days isn't possible for you in your season of life, then look for smaller windows where you can create space for yourself. How can you be intentional about the time when your kids are napping or at soccer practice? Some of my best memories from the North Shore are of the afternoons when I would retreat to my own room and lie on my bed while my kids napped. I could look out my window and see the top of a weeping willow in our backyard. I would lie there for an hour and let my mind wander over whatever big question I was facing. I didn't read. I didn't try to tackle the list of tasks that was always waiting for me. I just engaged with my brain in a different way.

No matter how difficult it seems to get away from the responsibilities and obligations that hold you in place, it's not impossible. Taking care of yourself is critical to taking care of those you love, and living as a whole and healthy person is one of the most precious gifts you can offer to those around you.

Whether it's two days or an hour, the most important part of a selah is to turn off all the outside noises. No TV, no books or magazines, and, most of all (and this is the hardest), no phone.

When was the last time you turned off your phone and put it out of sight? Today we're groomed to depend on our phones for almost everything. We can't get from our front doors to our cars without checking our apps. We can't get through lunch with a friend without replying to text messages. Dozens of studies have been made about the addictive nature of cell phones, and now there's even a word for the fear of being without a mobile device: nomophobia.[1]

All those outside bells and lights and messages are blocking your mind from being able to focus. So put away your phone. If you need something in your hands, pick up some colored pencils and draw or color. Bring a paper journal and a pen and write whatever comes to your mind. Or give yourself permission to do nothing but think.

Who am I when no one else is around?
What do I love?
What am I passionate about?
What am I longing to do differently in my life?

A selah is a chance for you to listen to yourself. I mentioned earlier that the key to this kind of deep, open thinking is discernment. That's a big word that essentially means filtering through garbage to get to truth. Discernment is about unpacking messages, challenging the ideas you've been living with your whole life, and finding your own wisdom. It's accessible to everyone, but it requires time and attention.

The image that I personally associate with discernment is putting piles and scraps of information on a table and sorting through all of it to find out how the pieces connect. Because I grew up in an environment where so much went unspoken, when I went searching for fragments of truth, I always felt like a sleuth. Discernment, for me, happens when I give myself time to put together the pieces of what I think, what I hear, and what I believe. It comes when I stop disregarding that nagging feeling I've had in the back of my mind or the check I've had in my spirit. It's what I find when I set aside my past as a wounded, disappointed, lonely child and see things as they really are. It's uncovering truth.

Other women describe their experience of discernment as feeling like they're all alone in a dark, quiet maze of hallways and using their senses to find their way through. They have to trust their inner sense of direction and the solid reality of the walls under their fingertips to guide them, even though they can't see the way.

Discernment isn't about judgment. It's not an excuse to start throwing harsh words at anyone, including yourself. Instead, it's a chance to ask the questions that have plagued your mind for years and find the thing that is holding you back, keeping you from experiencing the fullness of life. If you are brave enough to do that, then discernment is the gift that will help you see what to do next.

❦

Once you've found your quiet space and have set aside time for your selah, the real work begins, and it comes with a lot of questions.

>What are you unhappy about? When did you first feel this way? What made you feel this way the first time?
>
>If, ten years from now, your life is exactly the same, would you be happy? If not, what is preventing you from making a change?
>
>How will you respond to what you've heard here so far?
>
>If you had a general nagging sense of being unhappy or unfulfilled before you started reading, do you know why? What was bothering you?
>
>If you picked up this book feeling like everything in your life was going in the right direction, do you still feel that way?

If you've uncovered some challenging ideas, take the time to name them.

I'm not suggesting that you go looking for trouble. If your answer today is that you're genuinely happy, that's great. You're in a good season, and there's no need to go looking for problems when you're feeling good about your life. Put the book on the shelf and go have fun. This, too, shall pass. When a new challenge strikes and you start to see patterns emerge that you don't like so much, pull this book back down and dig in again. You'll know when it's time.

However, if there is something tugging at your heart, don't

gloss over it. Don't keep trying to treat the symptoms in your life, numbing yourself through various means without pushing deeper to understand the painful why.

Get started by asking yourself these questions:

OF THE FIVE EXAMPLES OF GROOMING IN THIS BOOK, WHICH ONE WAS THE MOST IMMEDIATELY UNCOMFORTABLE FOR ME TO READ? WHICH ONE SURPRISED ME?

When I've talked to women about the different ways we're all groomed, most of them immediately attach to something. "I'm angry with my church (or someone in my church) right now, so I must be groomed for judgment." Or "I'm exhausted trying to keep it all together, so the endurance message really spoke to me."

You're probably right when you identify those things, but remember that many of the messages are interconnected, and most women aren't affected by only one type of grooming. A selah is a chance for you to be open to the message that's less obvious but probably more influential. You won't see yourself in all five areas, or in all of my stories, but stop and ponder whether there's anything still below the surface.

IS THERE A SECRET FROM MY EARLY MEMORIES THAT I'VE BEEN CARRYING WITH ME?

Your mind may try to resist remembering this event in detail. That's a sign that it's trying to protect you, just as it has done for years. Don't let it. Give yourself time to draw out the details of the key moments that defined you, even the painful ones. What did people do or say? What happened next? Don't skim over the details. Freeing yourself of a memory involves being able to bring it out into the open. Put yourself back in those places and see what new things you notice.

IF I DO START TO CHANGE, WHAT ARE THE POSSIBLE COSTS? WHAT ARE THE POSSIBLE OUTCOMES? WHAT WOULD I HAVE TO GIVE UP, AND WHAT WOULD I GAIN?

It's super uncomfortable, I know. The fear of change is often greater than staying in your pain. But it's also super worth it.

IF I COULD CHANGE THREE OF THE EVENTS THAT HAPPENED IN MY LIFE, WHAT WOULD THEY BE?

There's no judgment here, so give yourself permission to be honest about the places where things might have gone off track. Maybe you wish you had spent more time doing something you loved. Maybe you wish you had married someone else. Maybe you wish you had tried to follow a dream or that you hadn't let your dream take you into certain dark places. Many of us wish we'd spoken up and objected when something happened.

WHAT ARE THREE THINGS THAT YOU CAN CHANGE TODAY ABOUT THE WAY YOU LIVE YOUR LIFE? WHAT'S STOPPING YOU?

This last question is critical because naming the things that stand between you and the life you want helps put them in context. As the saying goes, "Darkness cannot drive out darkness." If the things that stop you stay in the dark, unexplored and unacknowledged, they loom large.

Are you worried about how your husband will react? That you won't be able to pay your bills or afford the lifestyle you have now? That you won't know how to act? That people will judge you? Are you concerned about how your first steps into freedom will affect your children?

Simply naming the things that hold you back from fully expressing yourself will diminish their power. And trust me, when you allow yourself to see clearly—when you start to discern the influences of your life—you'll have the tools you need to follow your new path into a world of possibilities.

Are you ready? The choice is yours, and the selah is always waiting.

Chapter 10

RELEASE

If you paused after the last chapter and gave yourself time to selah, you may have acknowledged, perhaps for the first time, the extent to which outside messages and events groomed your life and journey. Those truths also may have uncovered some hard-to-process emotions.

Discovering layers of long-buried resentment when we look at the events that shaped us is common. Study after study shows that people with a history of trauma often remember sensory details—sounds, what something looked like, even smells—in shocking detail years later.[1] When you paused in a selah and let your mind be still, those memories may have come flooding back and hit you in a rush. You may have remembered exact words, or the specific expression on a person's face, or what that person was wearing. I may never remember the name of that guy in the frat house, for example, but I'll never forget his parachute pants. When I walk onto a farm and smell tractor oil, it brings me immediately back to the farm in Arkansas and the feeling of riding in that truck on the way to church. Laurie will always remember the exact words her mom used when she commented on her weight.

Those memories can play and replay, filling your mind and creating walls that continue to block you from living openly and honestly with other people.

When the girls first arrive at Selah Freedom, most of them are in that place. Their identities, their hearts, and their feelings are tied up tightly with the way they've been living and the messages that brought them here. That pressure affects them physically, mentally, and emotionally. They have trouble concentrating on anything in their futures because they're still hiding behind the emotional safeguards they put up to survive their pasts.

What's true for the Selah girls is also true for all of us. When we're caught up in our false messages and secrets, we have a hard time engaging with the life that's right in front of us. Every interaction with an innocent stranger has the potential to flash us back to a difficult message. Every quiet moment is full of loud memories. Creating a vision for the future is difficult with all those emotions pushing through.

That's why it's important that you not stay there. Once you've recognized what pieces of your story have been holding you back, the only way to move forward is to return to the person you were before those things were stolen from you.

For your own sake, you need to release.

That journey starts with letting go of any anger you're carrying, whether it's the long-simmering bitterness you've held for years or a current of outrage that recently exploded in your life.

If you're used to covering up your reactions, locking shame or hurt away in a box and never talking about it, those feelings didn't disappear with the passage of time. They're still there, a live bomb waiting for something to set them off—whether that's a changing relationship with an aging parent, a chance encounter with an old acquaintance, something you see in the news, or the stories you've read on these pages.

Right now your anger may seem like the only feeling that fuels you. Who would you be without it?

But getting mad isn't the same as getting healing. You can't let go of your secrets if you're still holding a grudge against the people who groomed you. Don't allow the person who hurt you to continue holding a piece of you—your heart, mind, or soul—through your anger. It's time to let that go.

But you don't know the terrible things she said to me.

You don't understand what he did to me in those dark rooms.

You're right. I don't. But I know that the only person who's being hurt by your lingering, festering anger is you.

There is a time and a place for outrage. Anger, as an emotion, is often the thing that protects us when we're in immediate conflict. It propels us to change. When we see that we've been wronged, anger covers the deeper responses of fear and sadness that get us stuck. I've seen hot flashes of anger finally motivate girls in Selah Freedom to walk away from their pimps, and I've seen it give suburban moms the strength to defend themselves and end relationships that hurt them.

But anger is just one step in the process of grieving. Once it has given you the strength to take action, it's time to move on.

Have you ever seen a stream clogged with fall leaves or some other kind of debris? What was once clear, bubbling water turns into stagnant mud with a layer of algae scum on top. When it stops moving, it becomes gross. That's true for us as well.

If you find yourself stuck in an endless loop of resentment or angry feelings toward a person who hurt you years ago, you're probably spending too much energy on something that can't be changed. If you notice (or, more likely, if a trusted friend points out to you) that you keep talking about the same wound, and the same person who wounded you, for years on end without any change, then your anger is holding you back and probably damaging other relationships.

You are constantly growing and changing. Your emotions must be able to move with you.

At a certain point, anger stops being the thing that drives us toward necessary change and starts being the thing that we hide behind. It transforms into bitterness and poisons our other relationships. If you grew up with divorced parents, you probably know what I'm talking about. The greatest pain comes not from the breakup itself but when one or both parents continue for years after the break to criticize and disparage the other.

It's time to let go of the things that are blocking your stream.

Let's talk about the flip side. While some women get angry when they think about their pasts, others continue to live deep in denial. They push away any negative feelings and do everything in their power to avoid the messy things that come up. These are the women who will never, ever talk about what happened.

But repressing the need to grieve isn't the same as healing. I remember a family who lived near mine when I was growing up. The father was an alcoholic who abused his kids physically and emotionally for years until one day he decided to get sober. Overnight this dad turned into a very present, very cool parent, and the whole family embraced his new attitude *without ever acknowledging that something had changed.* If I ever tried to talk to the kids about what had happened, they'd shrug it off. "Things are different now," they'd say. "We're not holding grudges."

The thing is, though, they weren't just "not holding grudges." They were pretending that those decades of fear and shame never happened. Today that dad's adult kids all struggle with various addictions. They have trouble holding steady jobs. Their marriages are fraught. When I talk to them, they're aware of their problems. They're constantly talking about how to break away from their bad habits. But I can't help noticing that they still never talk about where their issues came from. They never dig into the messages they heard as children or the ways they've tried to compensate for their early memories.

When we cover our emotions and refuse to let them out, we cut off our ability to grow past our grooming. It's tempting to say, "I don't want to feel all of this anymore, and I don't want to have these thoughts anymore, so I'm going to shut the gates and be done with it." But denial isn't the same as release.

I have another friend, whom we'll call Alexis, who is also stuck in this loop. Her dad sexually abused her when she was a child, a secret that she's never told anyone, except me. She says it's because she refuses to let what happened be part of her identity, but if you watch her carefully, it's clear that her past is still consuming her. For as long as I've known her, Alexis has been a whirlwind of accomplishments—an award-winning dancer in high school and college, homecoming queen, valedictorian, star employee, marathon runner, and PTA president. She strives to define herself with every role she can find *as long as it's not the one that she thinks about every day.* When she interacts with her kids or sits in a rare quiet moment, you can feel the tension and fear radiating off her.

At Selah Freedom we always say that you need to go back to the root. Once you deal with the root, the fruit changes and the symptoms fall away. Denial is a cover you hide behind, just like the anger. And when you hold on to it for too long, it's just as damaging.

One of the girls I met through Selah Freedom told me that she'd been to seventy different intervention programs before she landed at our assessment house, but nothing had ever been able to break the cycles of her issues. The programs never got to the root of her pain. Her problem wasn't with drugs or alcohol; those were the symptoms of the enormous amount of psychological trauma she was carrying around.

If you've given yourself permission to go through the questions and processes of this book, the truth is out there now, and it won't be ignored. You can't keep covering, numbing, overscheduling, overworking, overeating, or whatever it is you've been doing to hide from the past.

To release something, you have to feel it all the way to the end. You have to let the experience be spent. Because a false ending isn't an ending at all. It's just a delay. Counterfeit.

If your overbearing mother picked your clothes, told you how to do your hair, didn't let you choose your own friends, and made all your other decisions too, it probably had a lasting impact on who you are today. You were groomed. Your identity was suffocated. And as you dig into that, you might discover that you need to grieve the child and teenager you never got to be. You may recognize layers of anger, long buried, springing from moments when you were forced into molds that didn't fit. You may also find some uncomfortable parallels in the ways that you're parenting your own kids, either repeating your mother's habits or swinging in the opposite direction to total permissiveness.

Several women I know report that the more they understood the ways they'd lost opportunities in their younger years, the more they emotionally reverted to those developmental stages. "I found myself snapping at my mother, getting sarcastic, and acting more like my middle school kids than a grown adult," one woman said. "Finally I cut off contact completely, and we didn't speak for years. My kids were devastated to lose their grandmother, but I just couldn't stand to be in the same room with her."

"I started judging everything in my life harshly," said another. "I would never have gone to that college or married that person or chosen that job if it wasn't for her. Everything hard or bad that happened to me for those years was her fault."

Do you see the problem with that approach?

When we hold on to the past, the negative effects of our emotions ripple out. Anger turns into bitterness, which sucks the joy out of everything. It leaves us mired in judgment and spreads resentment. Release frees us from all of that.

Release is about letting go of the past so that it doesn't still affect the way we live now. Who we are today is no longer tied to who we were back then. The things that happened to us no longer define us. Release means reclaiming our minds, our lives, and our futures from the negative messages that held us back. Release allows us to name what was stolen and who we were before it was stolen and to start doing the work that has to be done to get it back.

Please understand that release is different from denial. It's not healthy to pretend that something never happened or that it didn't affect you. You can't release what you don't acknowledge. Instead, release is about choosing to live in the present and future in new ways and rewiring those neural pathways we talked about in chapter 3.

That's easier said than done, of course. The process of release is an intentional, daily choice to look forward instead of back, but the outcome is worth it.

Today when I tell the girls at Selah Freedom my story, they're shocked. "You don't look like all of that happened to you," they say, eyeing me suspiciously. And it almost makes it all worth it when I get to smile at them and say, "Not anymore, I don't. And if you give yourself the chance, neither will you."

So where do we start?

Faced with the difficult pieces of our past and the ways that other people influenced and affected us, it's tempting to see only one side of the story. *Look what happened to me. See how that person groomed me to be what they wanted. Pay attention to everything I lost because of that.*

Naming our experiences and feeling their impact are both

important parts of the journey, but if you really want to be free, step back and look at the bigger picture. Your story, after all, is one part of a much larger narrative.

If you see places where you were groomed by people you trusted, can you also see why they did what they did? Have you ever asked?

If you had a controlling mother, like the woman I described above, how much do you know about her past? What was her story? What was she groomed for? Why was it so important for her to be involved in your life? Did something happen to her when she was young, so she spent her adulthood living in fear and trying to protect you? Or did she also grow up with strict parents and carry their parenting methods forward? Was mental illness, trauma, or something else out of her control involved?

Opening yourself to other perspectives is another kind of discernment because it helps you see more of the context around your story. It doesn't mean that you're trying to excuse or explain away the behavior of others; nor does it lessen the effects of someone's actions. This isn't about their guilt or innocence. It's about context.

One survivor I met told me the story of her father, who sexually abused and trafficked her for years when she was a child. He was eventually caught and convicted, and the woman cut off contact with him for many decades. Her pain and anger went deep, and she struggled throughout her adulthood to have healthy relationships.

When her father was in his eighties and dying, she went to his deathbed. While she was there, he told her about his own childhood. He had been thirteen when some older boys showed him pornography for the first time. "Do you like it?" they asked. When he said yes, they invited him upstairs to see more. He followed, but instead of pulling out more dirty magazines, the boys gang raped him. After that, the idea of sex was broken for him, and he became a predator himself, drawn to children whom he could abuse in a role of power, never again a victim.

Did hearing this story change those horrific years the survivor had experienced? Did it erase the memories of what her father had done to her? Of course not. But it did give her a new perspective on why things had happened to her. She could accept, finally, that nothing about the abuse she'd experienced was her fault.

We can discover empathy—understanding the feelings of others—without condoning or agreeing with anything we discover.

That survivor took a risk in inviting her abuser to share his story. That's not something that works for everyone, and it may not work for you. Some of you don't have the opportunity to encounter the person who hurt you. They're gone from your life, either through death or passage of time. But for those of you who have the opportunity, the question often looms large. Should you talk about all of this with the person who groomed you? Does the person who hurt you have any voice in your process of release and forgiveness?

For the girls at Selah Freedom, we counsel that once they've left their pimps, it's best to cut off all contact. They shouldn't give him their phone number. They shouldn't pop in to visit at

Christmas. If your perpetrator is a master manipulator or enjoys causing you pain, chances are nothing good will come from further communication.

But in the end, the answer to this question is entirely up to you. Each of you has a different story and a different relationship to consider.

Fifteen years ago, I sat down with my father and shared with him some of my memories and reactions for the first time. I did it not because I was particularly brave but because I'd given an interview to a magazine and shared parts of my story that he didn't know, and I wanted him to be prepared.

My relationship with my father has been tumultuous over the years, and I was worried about how he would respond. I expected him to be angry and to argue with me about how my experiences would affect his reputation. After all, that's how we'd always communicated before. But my dad surprised me. As I shared my story with him, his eyes were full of shock and then sadness. When I talked about my abortion, he cried. He later said he couldn't stop thinking that would have been his first grandchild. Would he see him or her in heaven, he wondered. The conversation was beautiful and extremely healing for me. It helped me see him on a different level.

One of the reasons that conversation went well, I believe, is I didn't try to change his opinions or memories, nor did I go in with an agenda. This wasn't about me telling him the ways in which I felt wronged. My anger had passed years before, and in that moment, all I wanted was for my dad to understand what it had been like for me to grow up. All I wanted was to be heard, and I was.

In many cases conversations like this, especially as you try to unravel complicated family dynamics, can bring you a new level of healing and understanding. It's important to note that I'm choosing the word *conversation* and not *confrontation*. If you're still struggling with anger and feel tempted to force an interaction and provoke a reaction, stop. It isn't a good idea. Initiating a conversation should never be an excuse to torture, ridicule, or persecute someone who hurt you. That won't bring the kind of broader perspective and healing I'm talking about. It won't help you find freedom.

But if you're trying to understand your past and you have an opportunity to have a conversation with a parent or other person of influence, it has the potential to give you new perspective.

If you're thinking about having a conversation with someone who groomed you, here are four important things to remember:

1. Frame it as a conversation and ask questions.

   How you set up this conversation will determine the emotional direction it takes from the beginning. Remember, this is an opportunity to listen and learn, as well as to speak.

   "Hey, Dad, I have a question for you about that time when the police came to the door because the neighbor thought that the fight you and Mom were having was getting violent. I remember how I felt so guilty at the time for letting them in and getting you in trouble. . . ." Then summarize the memory or moment, staying as close to the facts and as far from the emotions as possible. "That's how I remember it as a five-year-old, at least. Now that so many years have passed and I see how small five-year-olds are, I'd love to hear your perspective. What do you remember?"

By asking your groomer to tell the story of a shared experience first, you open the dialogue without accusations. The goal is to find points of compassion and understanding.

"Hey, Mom, sometimes I look at my daughter and think, *Wow, I really hate those jeans she's wearing.* Or *Oh my gosh, you look so bad in that dress.* And it's making me remember that when I was her age, you often had an opinion about my clothes. Where does that come from? Did your parents have opinions about what you wore?"

If your groomer doesn't respond well to your questions, shoots you down, or denies what you've said, don't keep pushing. Let it go. Conversations only work if both sides are willing to be there.

2. Manage your expectations. Your groomer probably has no idea how much you were affected.

When people go back to their parents or other early influencers and ask questions about their most vulnerable memories, it's amazing how often others' reaction is "I don't remember that at all." What you see as an important memory may not even register with them. Your groomer probably has memories of things you've forgotten too. And even if your significant person remembers the incident or habit that wreaked havoc on your life, it's unlikely to look the same in their memory as it does in yours. No one, after all, is the villain in his own story.

In the end the thing you may learn most is *My groomer wasn't intentionally trying to change my life.*

3. Slinging accusations and angry words won't bring release.

This goes back to the idea of having a conversation, not a confrontation, but it bears repeating. Don't go into this encounter with emotional guns drawn and anger burning. If you're upset already, there's not much the other person can do to assuage you, and putting someone on the defensive right away is the best way to have an argument that goes nowhere.

Wait until your anger settles, when you can go in with an open heart and a commitment to listen more than talk. In most cases, if you believe that your groomer loved you, then approach the conversation with the attitude that the person did the best he or she could with limited resources. (Again, it's not always appropriate to approach your groomer. If you don't have the underlying knowledge that the person cared about you, it's unlikely that you'll reach a resolution.) Keep the conversation focused on their perspective and memories. What can you learn?

4. You don't need an apology.

Don't go into this conversation with visions of a movie-worthy reconciliation. Because your groomer will probably not remember things the way you do, it's unlikely he or she will feel the need to apologize. What matters isn't whether your groomer shows remorse or even acknowledges your experience. You should have already worked through things enough to know what is true. What matters is that the conversation adds to your broader understanding of your past and allows you the space to bring out the things that were once secrets.

If you're feeling stuck in your own story but talking to the people immediately involved isn't possible, another way to break out of the negative emotions that consume you is to invite other, neutral observers into your narrative. Who else saw the things you did? A sibling? Another family member? A friend?

Forty years after my sister Diana's death, just as I was starting to write this book, one of her best friends, Debbie, found me on Facebook. I hadn't seen or heard from Debbie since Diana died, but I recognized her name and picture right away. She was the same age Diana was, and encountering her again was like seeing a vision of who my sister might have become. Debbie reached out to me with a long message, and we ended up talking on the phone for hours. She told me what she remembered about me as a six-year-old, and it was both painful and healing.

"Your sister would be so proud of you," she said, and I felt a piece of my heart heal.

Over the years I've gone to aunts and cousins to ask about our family's history and patterns. And I'm consistently surprised by how different people's experiences are, even when they're in the same space and time. That realization forces me to step back and ask if I'm seeing my own story clearly.

Seeking input from others like this should never devalue your perspective or your memories. Instead, it has the potential to add richness and nuance to your story, and it prepares you for the real challenge: forgiveness.

Elizabeth, no. That's going too far. This person doesn't deserve for-giveness. What happened to me is unforgivable.

I get it. I've heard stories from women who were groomed and abused by atrocious people. There aren't enough questions or stories in the world to help us understand truly sociopathic perpetrators. And like I said, I don't recommend seeking out conversations with people like that. You don't need to understand their motives.

But here's the thing: Forgiveness isn't something you do for the perpetrator. Forgiveness is something you do for yourself.

When you forgive, you break the emotional bonds that exist between you and the person who hurt you. Those painful events have controlled your thoughts for far too long already, and forgiveness is how you separate yourself from their influence. Forgiveness happens when your energy is no longer caught up in anger, or any feeling, toward the event in your past.

Forgiveness is about seeing a person who wronged you in a neutral light, as a flawed human being, and seeing a painful incident in light of your entire life story, as a piece of your past. This is a long, slow process that happens only over time.

This is a tough chapter, and it's asking you to do hard things. But every paragraph was written with one goal in mind: to help you change the ending.

When you seek to release yourself from the secrets and false messages of the past, you'll open the doors to a new way of life—one that's determined by you and not your groomers. When you find peace and honesty within your story, you're ready to take control of it and move toward the places you want to be.

So here's one final suggestion for finding release, based on what we've learned at Selah Freedom: *mark this moment of change and commitment to the future with an impact statement.*

This activity actually sprang, weirdly, from something we see often in the court system. When a pimp or sex trafficker is arrested and convicted, the judge allows that person's victims to come and make an impact statement. The girls at Selah Freedom spend weeks working on their letters, which they then stand up and read in front of the whole court. It's an empowering moment to witness, when the man who once controlled everything sits in handcuffs and the girl who was once under his control stands in freedom. I'll never forget one girl, who had gone through years of horrendous abuse, facing her trafficker with so much courage that the state's attorney called it the most powerful thing he'd heard in his twenty-year legal career.

We brought the idea of the impact statement back to Selah's residential programs, and it's also applicable to you in whatever situation of release you find yourself in. Here's how you can craft your own.

Write down what you want to say to the person who hurt you. (Put away your keyboard for this and write it longhand. The emotional power of seeing your own handwriting will make it deeper.) Write it as a letter to the person you need to release.

In your letter don't hold back. Name what was stolen from you. List the ways the person's actions affected you. Share what might have been and how those decisions from long ago have changed your life. Let it out. This is your chance to put all those feelings into words.

Then write how you're going to live now because you're not trapped by those messages anymore.

When you're done, decide if there's anyone who needs to hear what you've said. It's probably not the person you wrote to—again, that kind of confrontation rarely ends with the apology you desire. Many women instead read their letters to someone who is emotionally safe: a counselor, friend, spouse, or sibling. Others are content to know for themselves what it says.

Here's the most important part: when you're done, seal the letter closed to mark the end of the conversation, and then *burn it*. At Selah Freedom we host regular bonfires for the burning of letters like this, but a match and a trash can in your kitchen or on your deck will also do. Watch the words disappear, and with them the memory that's been taking up space in your mind for so long.

The person you were no longer defines you, and you can walk into any situation, any room, as a new person, free from fear and sure of your own worth.

It's time for the new you to begin.

Chapter 11

RELAUNCH

Almost twenty years ago I was pregnant with my daughter while I was in graduate school and doing my psychology practicum in a community health center in Chicago. We served an intense population, and it seemed like every patient I saw had some kind of sexual abuse in their history. I went to my supervisor one day, practically in tears, and asked her, "How will I protect my daughter from this? If this is the world we live in and these things happen, how will I keep her safe?"

My supervisor, a wise and experienced sage, shook her head. "You're asking the wrong question," she said. "It's not about how to protect her from the world. Rather, how you will be there for her when something happens because, chances are, something will happen. Maybe not directly to her, but close to her. The question is, will you be the mom who is ready to talk about anything—the mom she knows she can come to?"

That, looking back, was the start of it all. It's when I learned that it's not enough to recognize and release your own past. The

155

whole point of facing your secrets is to reach the place where you can put yourself out there and make significant, meaningful changes in the world around you.

It's time to break the cycle, take control of your future, and reach a place where other people see you and say, "Wow, you seem different. There's a softness about you, and a new strength. You seem more peaceful." Then it's time to tell them why.

A mentor of mine once told me, "People will tell you all kinds of things, but if you want to know what they're really about, watch their feet." In other words, what are they doing? What truths are they walking out in the real world?

As you've gone through this book, perhaps you've filled a journal, had a few hard conversations with yourself, and found a new level of inner peace. That's great. But now what will you do with it? How will you walk this out in the real world?

It's time to identify what those steps will be for you. Where are the places you've been letting your secrets and false messages define you, and how can you change them? For example, if you've been investing only in appearances, what are three specific things you can do this week to live a more authentic life? If you've been making decisions based on guilt or the fear of divine judgment, what is one thing you would choose to do differently if that was taken away?

Get specific about your plans. They don't need to be wild or dramatic. Most of you won't sell all your stuff or quit your job tomorrow. But choose something. Say no to the person who's been bullying you to host an event. Quit that committee that sucks you dry. Schedule a weekend away with just you and your husband. Sit down with your kids and talk to them about a piece of your story. Enroll in a class to learn that skill you need.

Let your family know that you expect them to pitch in more often and delegate specific tasks. Commit to a single month of sobriety.

This is your relaunch, and I can't wait to see how you use it.

This relaunch step is important. Taking what you know and acting on it, revealing your true self to the world, may seem scary at times, and it will be tempting to cling to behaviors and thoughts that are familiar even if you know they're not beneficial. But that's not going to work anymore. If you keep knowingly and intentionally making decisions because of the negative things that happened to you in the past rather than acting in a way that supports the person you're moving toward becoming, you'll end up living like a victim.

Victim is a word I hear a lot. When most people talk about the millions of girls lured into sex trafficking every year in the United States, they call them victims, and I understand why. These girls are not perpetrators. They are the people whom perpetrators abused. They were coerced, tricked, bullied, or forced into the sex trade, and they deserve compassion and support, not punishment.

In spite of that, though, at Selah Freedom we do everything we can to avoid calling anyone a victim. That's because we've seen how the word can become a label that's easy to hide behind, and how it can sometimes grow into a permanent identity. When a woman sees herself as a victim, she can get stuck in the past, believing the worst possible things about herself and thinking that what happened will always define her. She struggles to see the control she has over her own situations and circumstances. A woman who lives under the label of *victim* is more likely to think of herself as helpless, fragile, and at the mercy of others. Her past can be wielded as an excuse for her present struggles, and she sinks into feelings of worthlessness and despair. In her vulnerable state she also continues to attract groomers who are looking for victims and too often finds herself in more powerless positions.

No one should live bound to the labels of their past.

Instead, we tell the girls at Selah Freedom that as soon as they walk through our doors, they are *survivors*. Their season of being used and abused is over, and they are among the few who were strong enough to live through it. We remind them that every cell in the human body replaces itself every seven to ten years. Our bodies are actively shedding the past every day, so it only makes sense that our minds, hearts, and decisions should be capable of reinvention as well.

I love the quote, often attributed to Paulo Coelho, that says, "Maybe the journey isn't so much about becoming anything. Maybe it's about un-becoming everything that isn't really you so you can be who you were meant to be in the first place." Everything, we tell our girls, begins now.

We share the statistics with them: how many women in America are abused, how many end up on the street, how many times the average woman is sold for sex, and how many of them don't live long enough to make a choice to leave. "The fact that you're here on the other side of all of that," we say, "with an amazing, beautiful future spreading in front of you, makes you one in a million. Nothing that happened to you was your fault, and it doesn't need to define you ever again. *Victim* doesn't come close to describing you, and we can't wait to see what you will do now that you've survived."

It may seem like semantics, but from our experience, the change in wording is critical. Victims can't see past what happened to them. Survivors put the past behind them and relaunch themselves.

I could choose to live my life as a victim—molested, raped, addicted, abandoned, divorced. Perhaps the things you've lived through could leave you with the label of *victim* as well. But what good would getting stuck there serve?

In no way do I want to minimize your experience, but when you learn to separate who you used to be and who you can become, you free yourself from the danger of repeating the past. True healing comes not from getting stuck in the cycle of your experience but from pointing it outward into the world.

The first thing to know about your relaunch is that it's almost impossible to do alone. A lot of the work you've done so far in this book has been internal, with just you, your memories, and your discernment. But if you're going to take the lessons you've learned and put them into practice, you're going to need some help.

If your questions and reflection brought up bigger issues, I encourage you to seek out a professional. Counselors and therapists trained in trauma, such as Dr. Q., can help you work through overwhelming situations.

Formal support groups are also huge helps for some people, especially if you're working through issues related to substance abuse or addiction. My aunt and uncle started taking me to Al-Anon meetings when I was eleven to address things that had happened in our family, and I was fluent in the Big Book and the Twelve Steps. As a young adult, I went to other groups to deal with some of my issues before I found the healing I needed.

In my experience, groups like this provide a safe space to explore topics that might come with layers of shame because everyone's there for the same reason. Every group is different, and it may take a few tries to find the one that works for you, but this is a helpful way to deal with the symptoms of your past.

The primary purpose of connecting with others, whether medical professionals or support groups or good friends, is acceptance and accountability.

Human beings can talk ourselves into—or out of—anything. Ask anyone who's joined a gym as a New Year's resolution only to quit before February; our intentions are often bigger than our willpower. Have you ever had a friend share the things she wants to do but then she never does them? Over and over you hear her express her desires for better friendships, better health, more education, or a fresh start, but oftentimes it's just talk. Listening to her can become incredibly frustrating.

When I was a volunteer at our church in Chicago, one of my roles was to serve as a kind of emotional emergency room. I was the first place people could go if they needed some sort of emotional help. I would hear their stories of pain and fear and anxiety, and my heart would hurt with them. I found out about so much pain that was hiding in my own neighborhood.

After we talked for a while, I would ask them questions: What are you going to do about this? What are the options you're considering? How would you like to take this forward? My job, in part, was to help them create movement and offer viable possibilities for change.

It was a hard lesson for me to realize how few people I met did anything. I would see them at a neighborhood cocktail party three weeks later, and they'd pretend that we'd never talked.

It was one thing to share their stories; it was another thing to take initiative for change.

Having the desire to make a change or do something different isn't the same as following through. Starting to change isn't the same as consistently doing it over the long term. That's why, when you're ready to relaunch your life, you need a special, designated support team who will challenge you to look at the world through new eyes and keep you accountable not to fall into old patterns.

But Elizabeth, I don't want to be a burden on anyone. I've got the book. I've got my journal. I'm fine on my own.

Actually, you're not.

Remember what we said about neural pathways back in chapter 3? Those deeply ingrained memories are like tire tread marks left by a car that's been spinning in the mud, often for years. Our opinions and reactions are set, and without some outside help, they're not going anywhere. But when someone comes and spreads sand or some kitty litter around our muddy tires, we gain the traction needed to back up and go a different way. When someone you trust asks the tough questions ("Are you okay with that?") or shares their own experiences openly, they give you a different perspective on your situation.

You need relationships that will hold you accountable for taking the ideas you've uncovered here and putting them into practice.

For example, if you know that you were groomed for invisibility, your support group will be the ones who ask your opinion and encourage you to volunteer your wisdom. They'll show you over and over how valuable you are, but they also won't let you get away with hiding your wisdom. If you know that the dramatic conflicts of your childhood have left you reluctant to act, willing to endure anything in silence rather than provoke an outburst, a supportive friend will remind you to carve out time for yourself and say no once in a while.

Are there already people whom you trust to speak into your life this way? Do you have friends or family members whom you can call on to speak with total honesty? For many of us, the answer is no. Sure, we have lots of casual girlfriends who will meet us for coffee or chat in the break room or carpool line. We post and share with hundreds of people a day online. But there's no real vulnerability in that. For you to discover lasting life change, you'll need to open up, shed some tears, share your questions, and then really, truly listen. Relaunching yourself takes two-way relationships that can't be replicated on a screen.

If you don't currently have honest, supportive friendships, or if you're not sure how to start a conversation about deeper things, one way to get started is to encourage your group of friends to read this book together and talk about one chapter at a time. I grew up in a church community that emphasized small groups and community gatherings, so I've been in programs like this all my life. I love book groups and discussion groups because when you get a bunch of women together, the stories and ideas start popping like popcorn. One person might be feeling stuck, but then someone else says something, and it's like a lightbulb turns on. "Oh my gosh, I've never thought about it like that, but you're right. What you just described about your life is just like what I'm struggling with." The healing happens all over the place. But it doesn't have to take place in a book group, and it doesn't have to be organized through a church, and it doesn't even have to start as a conversation about the specific topics in this book.

What's most important is that you start to create space for real, honest, vulnerable conversations with other women. You may start to meet other moms on the playground on a regular day and talk while the kids are on the swings. You may be in a workout group and invite a few women out for coffee after. Maybe there's a discussion group or self-help book club at your local community center or bookstore.

I believe that every person has a certain frequency, like a radio station. The more we know who we are and the more we develop our interests and beliefs, the louder our frequency gets. Eventually someone with a similar frequency will tune in to us.

Wherever you are, be prepared to bring your vulnerable, honest self to the table. If all you do is complain about traffic and gossip about the latest school fund-raiser, you won't discover the depth of friendship that's possible. When you're sitting next to the friendly looking woman at your kid's soccer game, drop a sentence or two into your conversation: "Oh, I've been reading this book about . . ." Or "I've been trying to get away for a quiet retreat for a day." Not everyone will respond.

Not everyone will want to talk about deeper things. But someone will, and that's the person you can invest in.

↩

Another way to gather support is through a personal advisory board. This is a term I borrowed from the business world. Selah Freedom has a group of advisers who have special knowledge in certain areas and who have expressed their willingness to be "on call" as subject-matter experts when the organization is facing a specific question. We have advisers in construction who help us plan our safe houses, accounting experts who help us navigate tax rules, psychologists who help us develop effective outreach programs, and many more.

What works for an organization also works for people. Some people call these sage voices advisers, and some call them mentors. From the beginning of my personal journey toward healing, I've intentionally sought out individuals who have wisdom in areas where I know I need to grow. Today there are about half a dozen people whom I can call when I have a personal question or decision to make. Some offer spiritual depth, relational knowledge, or protocol with social skills and leadership. Others help me with parenting and practical planning skills.

Of course, my personal advisers aren't really a "board." They never come together to sit around a table and discuss my health and wellness or expect me to offer a PowerPoint presentation. In fact, I've never formally invited most of them to be mentors. They might be surprised to know I count them as such. But every one of them has changed my life.

One of my most precious advisers is a woman I met at a luncheon a few years ago. I didn't know her at all, but we were seated at the same table, and she seemed cool. She was ninety-two years old and stood out like a firecracker. So I asked her, "You seem like so much fun. Would you ever want to grab lunch sometime?" She said yes, and we started getting together every month or so. She's ninety-four now, and I drive over to her house whenever my parenting role gets overwhelming. Bernice will pull out the wine and cheese and then give me a chance to unload all my fears and insecurities. She raised three kids of her own while holding down a career and a beautiful marriage, so she gets it. She gets me.

Finding advisers or mentors doesn't have to be a big formal process. It can be like my friendship with Bernice, starting with a simple invitation to lunch and then developing. But it does require intentionality and vulnerability, and sometimes you'll need to take the initiative. I can tell you my gift of tears has served me well. I am not one of those women who always keeps it together. Sometimes when I call, all I can do at first is cry. That level of authenticity allows others to realize how much I trust them and value their speaking into my life.

Building a group of advisers takes time because not everyone has the specific knowledge and skills you need. But the more you look, the more you'll find the right people. You probably have one or two in your orbit already. If you're a mom, look at the other moms in your network. Especially if your kids are in school, you'll meet parents of all different ages and backgrounds, and some may have a few more years of experience in parenting or in life. If you're developing your career, look for networking groups of other women in your field. If you're part of a church or faith community, look for small groups or outreach projects that will connect you with other generations.

Cultivate those relationships. Do what I did and offer to take someone interesting out to lunch. Volunteer to help with a project where you can talk while you work. It may feel uncomfortable at first, but in my experience most people with a few years under their belts are happy to share what they've learned. And we miss out on so many cool opportunities if we're not open to letting other people observe our honest selves and speak into our lives.

Relaunching isn't just about building safety nets and accountability outlets for yourself, though. It's also about finding ways to use your own story to support the women who come behind you.

I had no idea, when I started this journey to uncover my secrets and overcome my grooming, where it would lead or what sharing my story would do. As I've said, it's certainly brought me to places I never planned. And then it brought me to Selah Freedom.

For the first year I lived in Florida, I was on a quest to do nothing except slowdown from my fast-paced Chicago life. When that ended, I went back to volunteering as a counselor and working through my own questions and issues. Then a friend from Chicago asked me to help organize a conference for women of influence.

To be honest, I wasn't all that excited about the event, but that still, small voice inside told me I needed to say yes. Something big would come from stepping out and getting involved. So I gathered a leadership team and started organizing committees. One of my jobs was to identify the official charity that the event would support. Philanthropy is typical at events like these, but we'd never discussed it in our early conversations.

I started asking the women in my community for suggestions of groups that we could help, and it was the first time anyone explained to me the realities of domestic sex trafficking. I had started working again as a volunteer counselor with women who'd experienced trauma and sexual abuse, a project that had been an important part of my healing and journey in Chicago, but until someone showed me, I had no idea that kids were being sold for sex just down the street.

Once the light was turned on, I couldn't look away. I started researching and learned about the three hundred thousand American kids sold for sex every year, most of them coerced within forty-eight hours of running away from an abusive home. I found out that they came from every zip code, race, and class. I was horrified to discover that my new home state of Florida had the third highest trafficking rate in the country and that my own metropolitan area had the second highest rate of trafficking in the state. My heart broke to think about how girls and boys were sold fifteen to forty times a day, typically for as long as seven years, and how many of them never survived to become adults.

"Okay, that's it," I said. "This is the issue for our event. Who do we write a check to?" But there was no one. No organization in our area, back in 2010, was dedicated to rescuing survivors of sex trafficking.

When I reported all of this to my committee, two women I didn't know well spoke up. Laurie and Misty had been drawn to join the team putting on this event even though they didn't have any particular interest in our topic. Their real passion was to help victims of sex trafficking. They'd been watching this issue develop for years, and they both were sure that they'd been called to open a safe house for trafficking survivors. But they had no idea how to fund it. Now here was the answer.

We agreed that I would speak from the stage to introduce the realities of sex trafficking to our attendees. As I prepared, it occurred to me that my whole life story had prepared me to help girls and young women who were sexually abused, and here where I lived were some of the most abused women in the country.

In 2011, I got on a stage in front of four hundred women and spoke about sex trafficking for the first time. The response was overwhelming. In 2012, we opened the doors of Selah Freedom. It grew quickly, with safe houses, outreach efforts, youth prevention programs, and global training. We quickly became the best provider network across the country. Today we serve thousands of girls every year with messages of hope, healing, and empowerment.

This is my stake in the ground, my commitment to using my story for good. Being honest about my story—the good and the bad parts, the pain and the grace—has opened the door for so many other women to explore their own and write their stories of redemption.

What's your story? When the time is right, I hope you'll feel empowered to share it.

At Selah Freedom, we like to encourage our graduates and supporters to "raise your hand and raise your voice."

Raising your voice means becoming comfortable with your own story and brave enough to share it when it needs sharing. It means setting aside the story you've carried in your head because that story you used to believe is gone. You've released it. But you still have pieces that you can use to write a new story, one that will help instead of hurt.

"A woman with a voice is by definition a strong woman," said Melinda Gates. "But the search to find that voice can be remarkably difficult."[1]

One of the most important things we offer the girls who go through the residential program of Selah Freedom is the chance to find their voices. Every one of our girls enters the program with a story in her head that she is damaged beyond repair, that she is useless, that she is disposable. But by the time she leaves, everything is turned around. She has discovered just how worthy, how loved, and how important she is.

After years of allowing others to speak truth and breathe life into them, these survivors are new people—pulled up, pulled out, and turned around. That's why when they graduate, we encourage each one of them to stand up and share their stories in front of the other residents and the staff. Attending those graduations is one of my favorite parts of the job because every one of those stories is amazing.

I'll never forget a girl we'll call Cassie, who came to us after years of being trafficked. Early in her life on the street, she'd gotten pregnant and had a baby, but she had lost custody because of her issues. On her graduation day, her grandparents brought her son, who was about six or seven at the time. Cassie got up in front of everyone and described how she'd come to Selah and rebuilt her life. She'd gotten clean, earned her GED, enrolled in college, and was working part-time as a barista. She had real friends, a plan to support herself, and a bright future.

When she finished, her son clambered onto her grandfather's lap to applaud. "That's my mommy!" he shouted, and there wasn't a dry eye in the house.

Your story, especially these most recent chapters of discovery, is a precious gift that can help others in similar situations. Are you ready to share it? Are you ready to let a stranger into your experiences to help her navigate her own complicated space? Do you see the value and importance of the place you hold in the world and how much of a difference you can make?

Once your journey of healing begins, if you aren't in some kind of reciprocal act of reaching out, then you're missing out. So say the thing that everyone's thinking. Speak your truth. People around you are longing for the opportunity to open up, and you could be the person who makes your circle safe.

I'm not suggesting that you post the details of your darkest memories on Facebook or call out a person who hurt you in front of a crowd of people. Taking the broadcast approach can easily drag us back into victim mentalities.

But take an honest look around. Is there anyone who needs to hear your story? Is there someone who would benefit from being asked, "Are you okay with that?" You might find them by raising your hand, becoming active in the area that once wounded you, the way I did through Selah Freedom. How will you pay forward what you've learned? Volunteer. Organize. Serve. Launch. Study after study shows that human beings thrive when they help others. Layer after layer of healing will come when you take your attention off yourself and start focusing on other people.

Is there something that's come up while reading this book that drives your passion? If so, there's a place where your wound is exactly matched to bring healing to someone else. For me, it was sexual abuse. For you, it might be income inequality and the challenges facing kids growing up in poverty. For my friend Linda, the challenge of raising two sons as a single mother led her to start a twelve-week parenting class at her local church, which grew into a full curriculum used across her county to help reunify families. Today GRIP (God Raising Incredible Parents) has helped more than one thousand parents learn practical and emotional skills, and it's all because Linda followed her passion and experience.

Your outreach might be getting involved with a local mentoring or tutoring program or offering professional development classes for single mothers so they can get better-paying jobs. If you have firsthand experience dealing with devastating diseases or special needs, perhaps this is the time for you to reach out to other families who are in the middle of that journey right now. Can you provide respite, care, or a listening ear?

Are you ready to be on someone else's advisory board? Can you step into others' lives and help them navigate the complicated physical and emotional landmines of crisis? Can you become the advocate you so desperately wanted when you were a child? I've never met a person who didn't long for a place where they didn't have to carry their burdens alone, and your helping hand might be just what they need.

For far too long you've seen yourself as the world sees you, not as who you are. But now things are different. You are more than a person under the influence of someone else or a feature of someone else's story. You are unique. You are important. Your own experiences are vital and essential to someone else's life.

And it's not just about you. The next generation of women needs you to break the cycles of secrets and shame. I've said before that if we keep our secrets, they will repeat in the next generation. Our daughters, nieces, granddaughters, and students are watching us, and they're using our experiences to guide their decisions.

Each of you will find a different outlet; what matters is that you step in and walk out the truth that you've uncovered. Redeem the dark corners of the story you've been given to change something for the better. When you are your true self, you will not be abandoned by those who love you. You will be welcomed. You will be embraced.

This book may have started with a secret, but it's ending with the truth. Within every secret lies your power and greatest realm of influence. I applaud you and can't wait to hear your true, beautiful, bold story!

ABOUT SELAH FREEDOM

Selah Freedom is a national organization with a mission to end sex trafficking and bring freedom to the exploited through four sustainable programs with proven results: Advocacy & Awareness, Prevention, Outreach, and Residential.

In 2010, Selah Freedom's founders—Elizabeth Melendez Fisher Good, Laurie Swink, and Misty Stinson—discovered the horrifying truth that local children were being bought and sold for sex right in their own communities. Sexual abuse, the root cause of sex trafficking, was targeting innocent children in every zip code in the United States.

The organization they started as a grassroots initiative has since flourished into a nationally renowned anti–sex trafficking service provider. They provide a network of safe homes and support groups designed specifically for survivors who walk through life-changing restoration and healing that many never knew was possible. The heart of Selah Freedom is to bring light into the darkness of sex trafficking and help survivors discover their inherent value and identity. The survivors the organization serves have believed lies about their worth and purpose since childhood. Selah Freedom works tirelessly to expel the lies, reveal the truth, and help them live a life free from shame and secrets.

From the success of Selah Freedom, the Selah Way Foundation emerged. This collaborative network of care unites the best practices from across the nation and engages donors with opportunities to make coast-to-coast impacts and save the next generation from the plight of exploitation.

Through three initiatives—Prevention, Protection, and Provision—the Selah Way Foundation works to get life-changing curriculum, customized for K–12 and interveners working with youth, into the hands of every child in the United States; train first responders so they can rescue victims and prosecute criminal traffickers and buyers; and provide a safe place of healing for survivors.

As the first two initiatives grow, Selah Freedom hopes eventually to discontinue the need for safe housing. Raising up first responders to be the protectors they desire to be, equipping children and parents with the tools they need to recognize the tactics of predators and speak up for their peers, will ultimately eradicate sex trafficking and exploitation altogether and help Selah Freedom reach its goal: to create a world with eyes wide open to this issue hiding in plain sight—a world where no child is sold.

Learn more at www.selahfreedom.com and
www.theselahway.org

ACKNOWLEDGMENTS

In the summer of 2009, people began telling me that I would write someday—not just one book but many. Long before Selah Freedom, and even longer before I could see how it would all fit together, they filled me with words of affirmation and assured me that I had many stories that needed to be told. The foundation of my story was already there, but I thought I was moving to Florida from Chicago to do nothing; I had no idea how strategic that move was. I wanted to rest and maybe relaunch, but primarily rest—to take my own selah! But my friends saw that God had different plans.

Again and again I heard that my story would touch people, especially women, in the deepest places of their souls. I never realized until recently how my entire life groomed me for the position I hold and the passion and authority from which I can speak. I thank God that every bit of pain, fear, and loneliness had purpose, and the full picture is just now coming into Technicolor clarity!

More than anything, I have such gratitude to our great God, who saw each part and patiently, and with extreme kindness, waited until I was in position to piece it all together to share all I have here.

The courage of my family to survive so many immense losses and still dance, celebrate, and love astounds me. I have more love and admiration for my mom, dad, and brother than mere words can express. How do you live through the unimaginable and still plug into beautiful moments? My extended family is one of the most resilient crews you will ever find. Each has walked with me as a hero during a different chapter of my life. We lived and learned the hard way, and nothing warms my heart more than the unbreakable love and loyalty that still live between us all. We're resurrected to a new level as we grow in age, wisdom, and gratitude.

My world would be unimaginable without my friendships. Jill Mursewick, you spoke vision into me and challenged me to see myself through your eyes and the eyes of God, beyond what I could have imagined. So much of what you saw in 2009 has come to pass. I'm in awe of your faithfulness. Beth Rech, my sister in spirit, for almost twenty years now, you have shown love in a sweet, gentle way. No games, no hoops or challenges, you are always there to rub my feet or massage my tired head. Forever a warrior and friend, Loretta Jacobs, you have the heart to love and love again. Thank you for your ability to fight for a friendship and see how wounds play a role. Roland Jacobs, who saw the Selah Way Foundation long before anyone else (especially me), I'm amazed by you! Jeanne Malnati, you were the first to ask me, "Is that really okay with you?" You changed my life and launched Selah. Anita Scott Treiber, like me, you always have the courage to speak truth even when it doesn't endear you to others. Thank you for always saying what needs to be said even when others aren't as brave. And to one of my newer friends, the warrior Abby O'Neil, it was no accident that you entered my life when you did. You helped me stand, understand transitions, and know when to move on in so many settings. I adore your strength and heart.

I do life with an army of individuals committed to helping me advance my mission, personal growth, and health. You've taught me the truth of the line, "Lord, don't steady her platform, but teach her how to stand!" I am forever grateful for this unshakable front line who goes before me in prayer and hems me in from behind. Jill Mursewick, Beth Rech, Freddy and Annette Feller, Dr. Latonya Powers, Cindy Pentecost, and of course my sweet, sweet Lynne Jubilee Cummings.

I'm thrilled and still in awe that my inner circle now includes Bradley Good, my husband. Mr. Good, I have never experienced such pure, beautiful, unconditional love. Thank you for being my closest friend and telling me to write, for believing it was important, and for wanting to hear my heart. You are a gift I longed for but never dreamed I would have, and I thank God every day that I get to live with that love and intimacy.

Selah, let's just say, is not a world for the faint of heart. I have such love and admiration for my two cofounders, Laurie Swink and Misty Stinson. Wow, did we dig in for more than I think we ever saw coming! I love so many of the phrases that became our Selah language: *Forget about the bus; you're lucky to have a seat on the rocket ship. Don't worry about what seat. Just hold on and buckle your seat belt. This will be a bumpy ride, but you will never be bored!* It's amazing to see what happened with the vision we had way back in Venice in 2009. Thank you for your love and loyalty.

Stuart Moore, you helped build so many aspects of Selah Freedom and the Selah Way Foundation. Thank you for always asking me to share more. Even when you would bring me to tears, you drilled down to my heart and helped our vision come to life. I have immense gratitude and awe for your relentless dedication to helping us create the best organization possible. I know of no greater compliment than when, back in 2015, you wanted to meet me because we were the "Google of not-for-profit."

Chip McGregor, when I went to my first writing conference, as I listened to all the different literary agents speak, I heard you and thought, *He's the one.* I trusted that in time God would bring us together. And in his miraculous style, he did just that. I didn't know then what I would write or when, but I knew it had to be with you. Chip, thank you for choosing me and walking alongside me. You are an amazing gift of encouragement and vision.

To all at Thomas Nelson and the W Publishing Group, thank you for choosing me! I remember sitting with Brad when Chip called to say I was offered a contract, and both of our jaws dropped right to the ground. Again, you have fulfilled the desires of my heart. You are an amazing team; thanks for teaching me the ropes. So very thankful!

And to the talented Beth Jusino, I love how different we are and how you challenged me each step of the way. I wasn't sure about you at first. You're tough, and in you I met my match! But now I am your biggest fan. You made me think outside my normal pitch and storytelling mode. "Cast the net wider," you would say, as I tried to blend with your view. You are strong, talented, and gifted beyond words. How you take my stories and position every word is truly a gift from God. Thank you.

In every book I have ever read, it seems the very last paragraph of the acknowledgments reveals the deepest nugget of the author's heart. For me that is my three beautiful, amazing children. Samantha, Maximilian, and Leopold, just writing your names brings such joy to my heart! Every unique aspect of each of you is the greatest gift God has ever given me. You could not be more different from one another, yet each one of you holds such talent and strengths. There is no way you will ever know how deeply I pray and thank God for you daily. I am so in awe that I get to have a front-row seat to watch your stories unfold. Giving birth to and having the privilege of raising you three is seriously the greatest accomplishment of my life. I love you to the moon and back—a million times!

FOR FURTHER READING

Ready to dive deeper into your own story or looking for resources to help you move forward? Here are a few of the books that helped me on my own journey.

- *Daring Greatly: How the Courage to Be Vulnerable Transforms the Way We Live, Love, Parent, and Lead* by Brené Brown
- *Rising Strong: How the Ability to Reset Transforms the Way We Live, Love, Parent, and Lead* by Brené Brown
- *The 5 Love Languages: The Secret to Love That Lasts* by Gary Chapman
- *Necessary Endings: The Employees, Businesses, and Relationships That All of Us Have to Give Up in Order to Move Forward* by Henry Cloud
- *Boundaries: When to Say Yes, How to Say No to Take Control of Your Life* by Henry Cloud and John Townsend

- *Everybody's Normal Till You Get to Know Them*
  by John Ortberg
- *Soul-Healing Love: Turning Relationships That Hurt into Relationships That Heal*
  by Beverly Rodgers and Tom Rodgers
- *The Invisible Bond: How to Break Free from Your Sexual Past*
  by Barbara Wilson

NOTES

INTRODUCTION: HOW DID I END UP HERE?

1. Based on data provided by the Clearwater Task Force and others. See "Facts and Stats," About & FAQ, Lauren's Kids, https://laurenskids.org/awareness/about-faqs/facts-and-stats/.

2. Melissa Hall and Joshua Hall, "The Long-Term Effects of Childhood Sexual Abuse: Counseling Implications," VISTAS Online, American Counseling Association, 2011, www.counseling.org/docs/disaster-and-trauma_sexual -abuse/long-term-effects-of-childhood-sexual-abuse.pdf ?sfvrsn=2; Elizabeth Hartney, "The Cycle of Sexual Abuse and Abusive Adult Relationships: Why Sexually Abused Children Grow Up to Have Abusive Relationships," verywell mind, updated May 4, 2019, www.verywellmind.com/the-cycle-of -sexual-abuse-22460.

CHAPTER 1: THE SECRETS WE KEEP

1. Hall and Hall.

2. Michael Slepian, E. J. Masicampo, Negin Toosi, and N. Ambady, "The Physical Burdens of Secrecy," *Journal of Experimental Psychology: General* 141, no. 4 (November 2012):

619–24; *Columbia Business School Archive*, www8.gsb.columbia
.edu/researcharchive/articles/6401.

CHAPTER 2: THE MESSAGES WE HEAR

1. "Understanding the Issue: Tools to Fight Sex Trafficking," *Selah Freedom*, www.selahfreedom.com/statsandresources.
2. One example: "Young Children Are Especially Trusting of Things They're Told," *Association for Psychological Science*, October 14, 2010, www.psychologicalscience.org/news/releases/young -children-are-especially-trusting-of-things-theyre-told.html.

CHAPTER 3: THE STORIES WE TELL

1. Brené Brown, "The Midlife Unraveling," *Brené Brown* (blog), May 24, 2018, https://brenebrown.com/blog/2018/05/24 /the-midlife-unraveling/.

CHAPTER 5: GROOMED TO BE INVISIBLE

1. Gary Chapman, *The 5 Love Languages: The Secret to Love That Lasts* (1992; repr., Chicago: Northfield, 2015).
2. Phoebe Stone, *The Romeo and Juliet Code* (repr., New York: Arthur A. Levine Books, 2012), 83–84.

CHAPTER 6: GROOMED TO ENDURE

1. Laura Zera, "No One Helped My Mentally Ill Mother, or Me," *New York Times*, June 22, 2018, www.nytimes.com/2018/06/22 /well/no-one-helped-my-mentally-ill-mother-or-me.html.
2. Henry Cloud and John Townsend, *Boundaries: When to Say Yes, How to Say No to Take Control of Your Life* (Grand Rapids: Zondervan, 2017), 29–30.

CHAPTER 7: GROOMED FOR JUDGMENT

1. Throughout this chapter, I talk about "churches" and "pastors," which are the familiar phrases of my own background and early messaging in Protestant Christianity. But no faith tradition is

immune from the human element, and so false messages and painful secrets are everywhere.

2. Chet Weld, "Pastoral Infidelity: Problems and Solutions," Crosswalk.com, December 26, 2011, www.crosswalk.com /church/pastors-or-leadership/pastoral-infidelity-problems-and -solutions.html.

3. Sarah Pulliam Bailey, "Southern Baptists Grapple with a Leader's Comments Encouraging Women to Stay with Abusive Husbands," *Chicago Tribune*, May 7, 2018, www.chicagotribune .com/news/nationworld/ct-southern-baptists-leader-comments -20180507-story.html.

CHAPTER 8: GROOMED FOR FINANCIAL FEAR

1. Mark Fahey and Nicholas Wells, "Americans Think About Money and Work More Than Sex, Survey Finds," September 9, 2015, BETTER, www.nbcnews.com/better/money/americans -think-about-money-work-more-sex-survey-finds-n424261.

2. Donna Partow, "Poverty Mindset—3 Signs You Are Being Held Back from God's Best," *Donna Partow* (blog), https: //donnapartow.com/poverty-mindset/.

3. Author's paraphrase of Ralph Waldo Emerson, *Emerson in His Journals*, Joel Porte selected and edited (Cambridge, MA: Harvard University Press, 1982), 377.

CHAPTER 9: SELAH

1. For a sampling of recent studies, see José De-Sola Gutiérrez, Fernando Rodríguez de Fonseca, and Gabriel Rubio, "Cell-Phone Addiction: A Review," *Frontiers in Psychiatry* 7 (2016): 175, published online October 24, 2016, www.ncbi.nlm.nih.gov /pmc/articles/PMC5076301/.

CHAPTER 10: RELEASE

1. One example: Jacek Debiec, "Memories of Trauma Are Unique Because of How Brains and Bodies Respond to Threat," *The*

Conversation, September 24, 2018, https://theconversation.com /memories-of-trauma-are-unique-because-of-how-brains-and -bodies-respond-to-threat-103725.

CHAPTER 11: RELAUNCH
1. Melinda French Gates, remarks, Powerful Voices Annual Luncheon, October 16, 2003, https://www.gatesfoundation .org/media-center/speeches/2003/10/melinda-french-gates -2003-powerful-voices-luncheon.

ABOUT THE AUTHOR

Elizabeth Melendez Fisher Good is the CEO and cofounder of Selah Freedom and the Selah Way Foundation, which exist to prevent sexual abuse, exploitation, and sex trafficking of children. Her leadership has brought freedom to thousands of American children and young adults who have been rescued from the sex trade, and she has helped educate millions on the topics of exploitation and sex trafficking. Good speaks and trains internationally and is passionate about protecting our youth from the secrets of abuse that so many are forced to keep. Her family is her true pride and joy. She has three beautiful children and lives with her husband in Sarasota, Florida.

To learn more, please visit
FreewithE.com